*By Jan Glaesel*

*The Complete Method For Trumpet*

# IMPROVE YOUR GAME

ALL SCALES TRANSPOSITION & DEXTERITY STUDIES

*Volume III*

## INDEX - VOLUME III

| Exercise | Page |
|---|---|
| Title-Page | 1 |
| Index Volume III | 2 |
| Foreword & My story | 3 |
| How to use this book | 7 |
| Introduction to chapters | 9 |
| Wise Trumpet Tapas | 11 |
| All Scales | 12 |
| Major Scales & Triads | 12 |
| Minor Scales & Triads | 14 |
| The 12 Major Scales | 16 |
| The 12 Natural Minor Scales | 18 |
| The 12 Mel. Minor Scales | 20 |
| The 12 Harm. Minor Scales | 22 |
| Chromatic Scales I | 24 |
| Chromatic Scales II | 27 |
| Chromatic Scales III | 29 |
| Chromatic Scales IV | 32 |
| Moving Chromatic Scales | 34 |
| The Seven Modes. | 39 |
| The Seven Modes Introduction | 39 |
| The 12 Ionian Scales | 40 |
| The 12 Dorian Scales | 44 |
| The 12 Phrygian Scales | 48 |

| Exercise | Page |
|---|---|
| The 12 Lydian Scales | 52 |
| The 12 Mixolydian Scales | 56 |
| The 12 Aeolian Scales | 60 |
| The 12 Locrian Scales | 64 |
| Wise Trumpet Tapas | 69 |
| Octatonic & Wholetone | 70 |
| First Octatonic Scales | 70 |
| Second Octatonic Scales | 75 |
| The 12 Wholetone Scales | 80 |
| Glaesels Brainboilers | 84 |
| Glaesels Brainboilers - Major | 84 |
| Glaesels Brainboilers - Minor | 87 |
| Glaesels Brainboilers - 1/1 tone | 90 |
| 2 Alternativ Brainboiler Themes | 93 |
| Dexterity Studies | 94 |
| Dexterity Studies - Level I | 94 |
| Dexterity Studies - Level II | 103 |
| Dexterity Studies - Level III | 113 |
| Musical Treats | 118 |
| Etude For A Mentor | 118 |
| Etude Pittoresque - E minor | 120 |
| Etude For A Friend - C minor | 122 |
| My Bookshelf | 124 |
| Credits | 125 |

COLOPHONE: TITEL: IMPROVE YOUR GAME - VOLUME III · 1. EDITION · AUTHOR: JAN GLAESEL · PUBLISHER & COPYRIGHT: JGMUSIK APS · DK 2012 · ISBN: ISBN 978-87-92945-02-0 · LAYOUT: AJOUR GRAFISK DESIGN · COVERPHOTO: HANS OLE MADSEN · WEBSITE: WWW.TRUMPETGAME.COM · CONTACT: INFO@TRUMPETGAME.COM

## FOREWORD:

This is actually the second time I'm writing this foreword. Right now I'm sitting at Starbucks in Central Pattaya, Thailand. I've just spent the last two weeks here in solitude in this wonderful country, away from home, work, phones and daily decisions, to finally finish my Trumpet Method Book "Improve Your Game – The Complete Method Book for Trumpet"

This project started in 2004, and the first time I wrote this foreword was in 2008 somewhere in the airspace between the U.S. and Denmark. I had been working in Las Vegas as a musical director for one of my Danish friends, a musical show genius, who wanted to try things out "over there". In my spare time, I collected all my notes on practising into one huge pile, and then thought, "That's it – the book is done". But boy was I wrong. When I got back home, I started looking at my "new book" – and it was a complete mess. It took me another four years to complete this project, inventing new systems and exercises to make the project come together. Now I have a complete overview of my material, have tried most of my ideas on myself, and now feel confident knowing that I have something of real value to pass on to my fellow trumpet players.

## HERE IS MY STORY:

While playing drums at the age of 6 in the Tivoli Boys Guard in Copenhagen, I practised the trumpet, and 8 years old I got my spot in the marching band and just fell in love with the instrument. I spent 10 years in Tivoli and by the time I retired at 16 years of age, I was a semi-professional musician. I could sight-read music, follow a conductor, learned to be on time, and learned all of the other things that make you successful in the business. But suddenly, I was "unemployed".

In high school I joined some different bands playing all different kinds of music. In the beginning I had a huge problem: There was no music to read!!! My whole life I had played from written music, and now suddenly I had to just play something and improvise. I was completely lost for a while, but with time came the courage to jump without a parachute. It sounded awful, and other trumpet players would probably have been kicked out of the band (unless you had a van or a rehearsal room), but I had something else. Due to my training in The Tivoli

Boys Guard, I had the power and technique to play all the high stuff, and I could play for hours without getting tired. On top of that I knew my theory, and had a flair for composing and arranging. So, whenever somebody needed an arrangement or song – they knew who to call. I stayed in business and started getting a lot of work. In 1979 I had the fortune to be approached by the Big Band Guru Thad Jones, who at that time lived in Denmark wanted to form a Danish/American big band - Eclipse. For the next 3 years I learned everything about being a big band section-player. That was an experience of a lifetime.

To cut a long story short, I ended up as Musical Director on Danish National TV and was placed in charge of some of the biggest acts in the entertainment business in Denmark. I became known as the guy who could play trumpet with one hand, and conduct with the other – and actually I can. I formed my own company writing music for feature film and commercials – boy I've written a lot of those.

A day is only 24 hours – that's a fact. So with a schedule as busy as mine has been for the last 20 years, I of course had to cut some corners. Since practising didn't pay bills, and wasn't fun – I cut down on that. For many years I never practised. I just played, played and played, because I didn't have the time to invest.

## THIS WAS THE WAY IT USED TO BE

After months of preparation, writing, rehearsing and just minutes before the first downbeat on the opening night of a show, I would ask the band: "Has anybody seen my horn?" I would find it, oil the valves and just give it a kick in the #¤%&, and would (barely) survive that first night. After a couple of shows it would get easier, and no one would suspect that I never practiced. The truth of the matter was that if you had given me a simple Danish Folksong and asked me to play it mezzopiano – I would have tanked completely.

## THE CROSSROAD

By 2004, we had played thousands of shows during a 15 year period so we decided to take an indefinite break. This wasn't a big problem for me as I had all my writing, arranging and producing jobs. BUT – what about my beloved trumpet? Now I had two options:

## SELL MY HORNS – OR – START TO PRACTICE!!

This book is the proof of my decision. The way back to falling in love with my instrument again has been long, frustrating, and hard, but above all – really, really rewarding.

## THE FIRST DAY AT "WORK"

After making the decision to find out how good a trumpet player I could have been, I started to practice. I had promised myself to practice at least one hour a day, and that sounded within reach for me. Then I experienced the scariest moment in my professional life. I went to my studio, got out the trumpet and stared at it for a loooong time, not knowing what to play. I played some scales – enough to make an hour pass by. But when I looked at the clock, only 3 minutes had passed. I put down the horn, and gave up.

I've never been good at defeat, so the next day I found my very old copy of Arban's Complete Conservatory Method For Trumpet. The Arban had been the bible for me in the Tivoli Boys Guard. I knew my way around it, but it had been a long time since I looked at it. I put together a one hour program of exercises from the Arban book, and had a really hard time getting it together. On the negative side it soon occurred to me what a lousy technique I had, but on the positive side, I started to improve – fast. Nothing is more rewarding than when you put in the effort and start getting results.

At a lecture in Copenhagen, American Business Coach **Keith Cunningham** came with a statement that really was an eye-opener for me. He said:

## "IF YOU HAVE A TALENT, NO MATTER WHAT IT IS, AND SPEND 3 HOURS A DAY FOR 3 YEARS ON IMPROVING YOUR SKILLS, YOU WILL AFTER THOSE 3 YEARS BE IN THE TOP 100 IN YOUR FIELD - WORLDWIDE!!"

An average lifespan is roughly 700,000 hours and you only have to spend 3,285 hours of those to get in the top 100 worldwide. How easy is that!! OK – if you want to stay at the top 100 or get to #1, you have to put in a lot of additional hours – but you get the picture.

Since I restarted my practice career, I've studied a lot of books from great brass players, including Allen Vizzutti, Arturo Sandoval, Schlossberg, Clark, Herring, Stamp, Caruso, Claude Gordon – you name it. I also picked a lot of brains, met and played with some terrific trumpet players to get the material together that helped point me in the right direction, and I really want to share this research and material with you.

Let me get one thing straight:
## I CAN'T PLAY EVERYTHING I WROTE IN THIS BOOK!!!!

If I only wrote exercises that I could play – I wouldn't learn anything. But I'm getting there: hour by hour, day by day, exercise by exercise. The day I can play everything in this book, I will write another. Here is a promise to you. If you can play the "Lyrical Interval Etude" that I wrote and dedicated to Mr. Malcolm McNab (in Vol. 4) I'll write a new one dedicated to you. (I can't play it – yet)

At age 54 I'm all fired up about playing and practicing my horn and I'm planning on improving my game for the next many years. I can't tell you when I'll stop – and as long as the horn sounds a little bit better every day I pick it up – I'll keep blowing.

## JAN GLAESEL
Copenhagen, Denmark - 2012

## HOW TO USE THIS BOOK

This book has been divided into 4 separate and independent volumes so that you can dig into specific areas instead of having to buy one large book just for one section, such as "The 10 Daily Routines" or "All Scales".

- **Vol. I – Warm-ups, interval & Slurring Exercises**
- **Vol. II – Pedal-tones & Low Notes / The 10 Daily Routines**
- **Vol. III – All Scales / Transposition & Dexterity Studies**
- **Vol. IV – Tonguing / Target, Precision & Endurance /Performance / Melodies & Etudes**

---

## IMPORTANT!!

I've come up with three basic "rules" that apply to this book. They are:

## 1.    REST ALMOST AS MUCH AS YOU PLAY

Practising can be harder than playing a gig. When I started this journey, I would practise one hour a day. My mistake was that I played for a full hour without resting at all. So when 60 minutes were up, I was done, and after a couple of weeks my lips were like two bricks. If you want to practice playing your horn for one hour – you should practice for two hours. Get the idea? Rest is important.

## 2.    3 STRIKES AND YOU'RE OUT!!

This needs explanation. When you look through the book you will probably be a little intimidated over all the high notes and tiring phrases – don't be. All exercises are written so that every trumpet player on an intermediate level can benefit from them – as long as they practice using this **"3 strikes and you're out"** rule.

Whenever you reach your current range limit – **give it three attempts, then stop.** The next day you can give it a shot again. In a few days, you will experience that what was once impossible, is now a walk in the park.

Exercises like this are divided into two or three sections. If I state, "Don't continue beyond this point if not within your range", stay within you range a couple of more days, and it will come. Remember: **"Good Things Come To Those Who Wait."** And HEY!! If the whole high note concept isn't something interesting to you, don't go there!! Simply skip those exercises, and let your normal high C be the top of your range. Remember:
**"No note is so high, that it can't be played an octave or two down"**!!

## 3.   PUT AS MUCH MUSIC AS POSSIBLE INTO EVERYTHING YOU PLAY

Let's face it – 95% of these exercises are plain boring when you just look at them. But if you try to put as much music or feeling into them when playing, you can make them come to life. On top of that you should play everything with the most beautiful sound you can imagine. These two things together are essential for getting to the point where time just flies when you practice.

In the Chapter on **Performance in Vol. 4**, I will share with you hundreds of ideas that made sense to me about trumpet playing that I picked up around fellow trumpet players and the internet. I call this, "Spiritual Tapas". In this same section, a good friend and fellow trumpet player **Jon Gorrie** will give you an introduction to his book "Performing In The Zone" – a book all performers should read.

LAST RULES:
**"TREAT YOURSELF TO SOME OF THE ETUDES IN THE BACK OF EACH VOLUME"**
**&**
**"TAKE A DAY OFF FROM TRUMPET PLAYING EVERY WEEK!!"**
LET'S PRACTICE!!

## ALL ABOUT SCALES - IMPROVE YOUR GAME VOLUME III

You can't be a trumpet player and work on a professional level without knowing something about scales. I used to only know the basics, but the last couple of years have inspired me to learn about all facets of trumpet technique, including scales. During my journey I had a hard time finding books for trumpet on the subject. I found a ton of books for piano and guitar, so I decided that I would dedicate a good portion of this book to scales, written so that they fit the range of the trumpet. Here we go.

## THE MAJOR AND MINOR SCALES & THEIR TRIADS - PAGE. 14-15

These are absolute basics. I put it in just in case you forgot them. Both major and minor scales go around the circle of fifths.

## THE 12 MAJOR & MINOR SCALES: ONE AND TWO OCTAVES - PAGE 16-23

Exactly as I write above the exercise, these are "not too interesting, but necessary".

You can choose to play these exercises in two ways. Either you can read them all the way through, or as I recommend, just read the first couple of keys and then use your brain to figure out the rest. That way, the scales will stick in your mind, and before you know it, all keys will be played naturally. Remember the "3 strikes and you're out" rule. This goes for all scale exercises.

## CHROMATIC SCALE EXERCISES
## EXERCISE 1- 4 PG. 24-38

Chromatic scales are so easy to play on paper, but once you get into them you it's hard to see the forest for the trees. It's so easy to lose your bearings. "Where am I? How do I get down from here? What octave am I in?" These are all questions that can stop your flow, so start slowly. This is the best advice I can give you concerning chromatic scales.

## THE SEVEN MODES OF THE DIATONIC MAJOR SCALE - PAGE 39-83

Please read introduction og page 39

### GLAESELS BRAINBOILERS - MAJOR, MINOR AND WHOLE TONE - PAGE 84-92

These exercises are really good for your brain. I use them for practising transposition. It's always good to be able to move a phrase to another key, so this is the object of the exercise. Play the phrase in C and get it in your head. Again, here it's important to close your eyes and think the other keys once the phrase is in your mind. You may feel frustrated the first couple of days, but stay with it. It will pay off.

### TWO ALTERNATIVE BRAINBOILER THEMES - PAGE 93

Once you know the original Brainboiler Theme inside out, you can start working on these two alternatives. I only wrote them in C, so here you HAVE to use your head to transpose them :)

### DEXTERITY EXERCISES - LEVEL I, II & III - PAGE 94-117

"Repetition is the mother of skill" is a phrase that applies to many aspects of both music and trumpet playing. This exercise is inspired by Carmine Caruso's "Musical Calisthenics for Brass". I have just developed it further to include all other keys. The exercise should challenge you with repetitive fingerings that will develop your dexterity. My dexterity sucks because I'm left handed and I use my right hand on the valves. I have to practice complicated phrases a lot, so these exercises help me.

### TREAT YOURSELF WITH SOME OF THE MUSICAL ETUDES & STUDIES PG. 92 - 95

## LET'S GET GOING - AND REMEMBER THESE WISE WORDS:

# "HOW DO I GET TO CARNEGIE HALL?
# PRACTISE - PRACTISE - PRACTISE!! "
### QUOTE: SAADI

# WISE TRUMPET TAPAS - "PRACTISE"

Strive to reach complete technical liberation and enter the sphere of music

Practise in short spurts. Focus on a few bars or a reduced passage

Practise intervals slowly until you strike each note directly in its center

Practise all technical material musically

Practise Eb music on Bb-trumpet.

Do something else to fill the space while you are resting - internet for instance:-)

When practising, make sure the rhythm begins on the first beat - not after.

Read an upper register passage down an octave to develop ease and security

Finish with soft playing to fine tune the aperture.

Lean into the horn.

*Just in case you forgot!!*

# The Major Scales and Their Triads-Sharp Keys

### Please read "Introduction to chapters" for reference - see index

Clock-wise round the circle of 5ths.

# The Major Scales and Their Triads-Flat Keys

Counter-clockwise round the circle of 5ths.

*Just in case you forgot these talso!!*

# The Minor Scales & Their Triads-Sharp Keys

Clock-wise round the circle of 5ths.

# The Minor Scales & Their Triads-Flat Keys

Counter-clockwise round the circle of 5ths.

*Not too interesting - but necessary*

# The 12 Major Scales - One Octave

### Please read "Introduction to chapters" for reference - see index

# The 12 Major Scales - Two Octaves

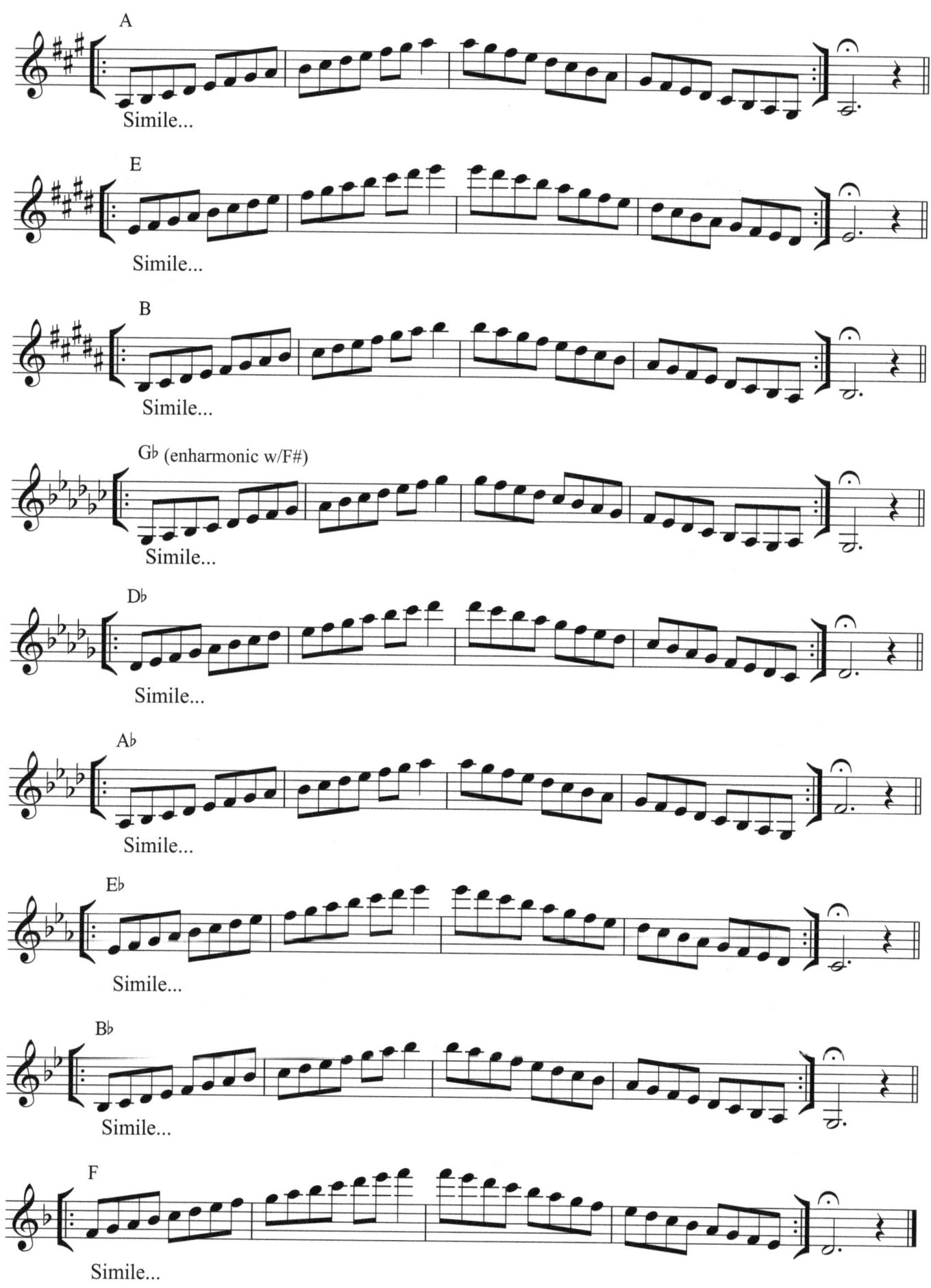

# The 12 Natural minor Scales - One Octave

# The 12 Natural minor Scales - Two Octaves

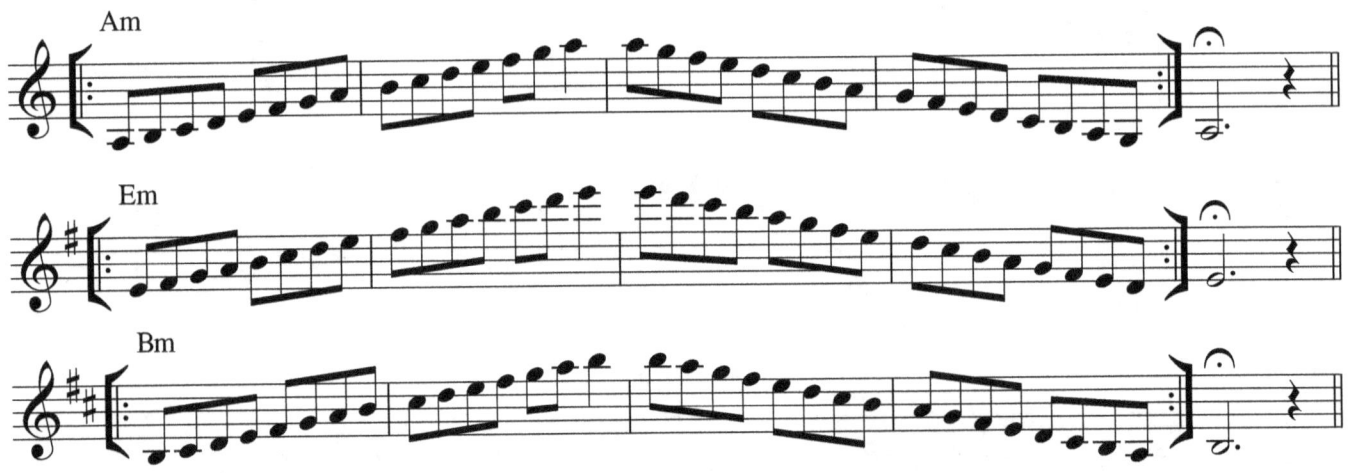

19

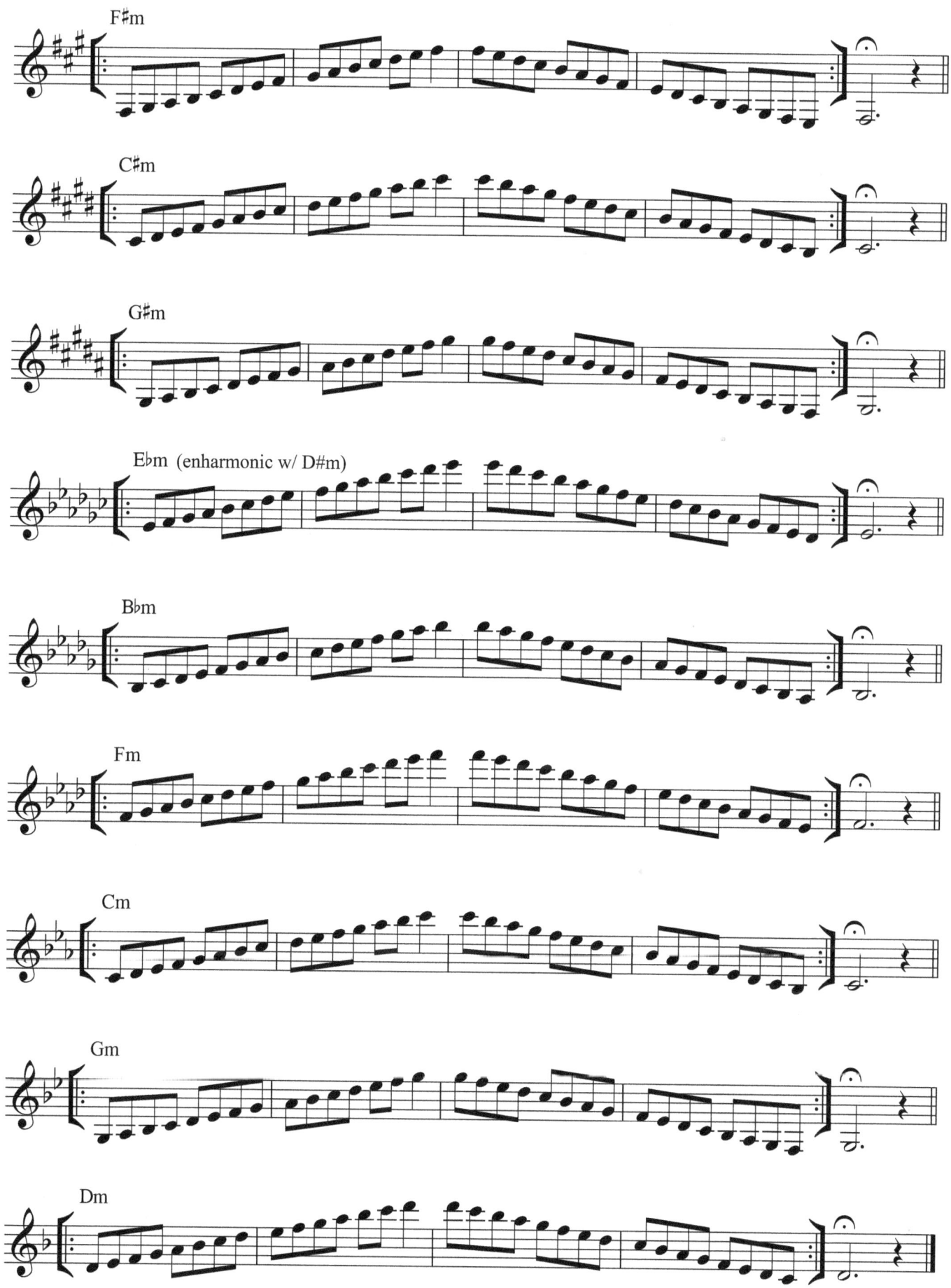

# The 12 Melodic minor Scales - One Octave

minor scale with raised 6th and 7th degree ascending, lowered while descending

# The 12 Melodic minor scales - Two Octaves

minor scale with raised 6th and 7th degree ascending, lowered while descending

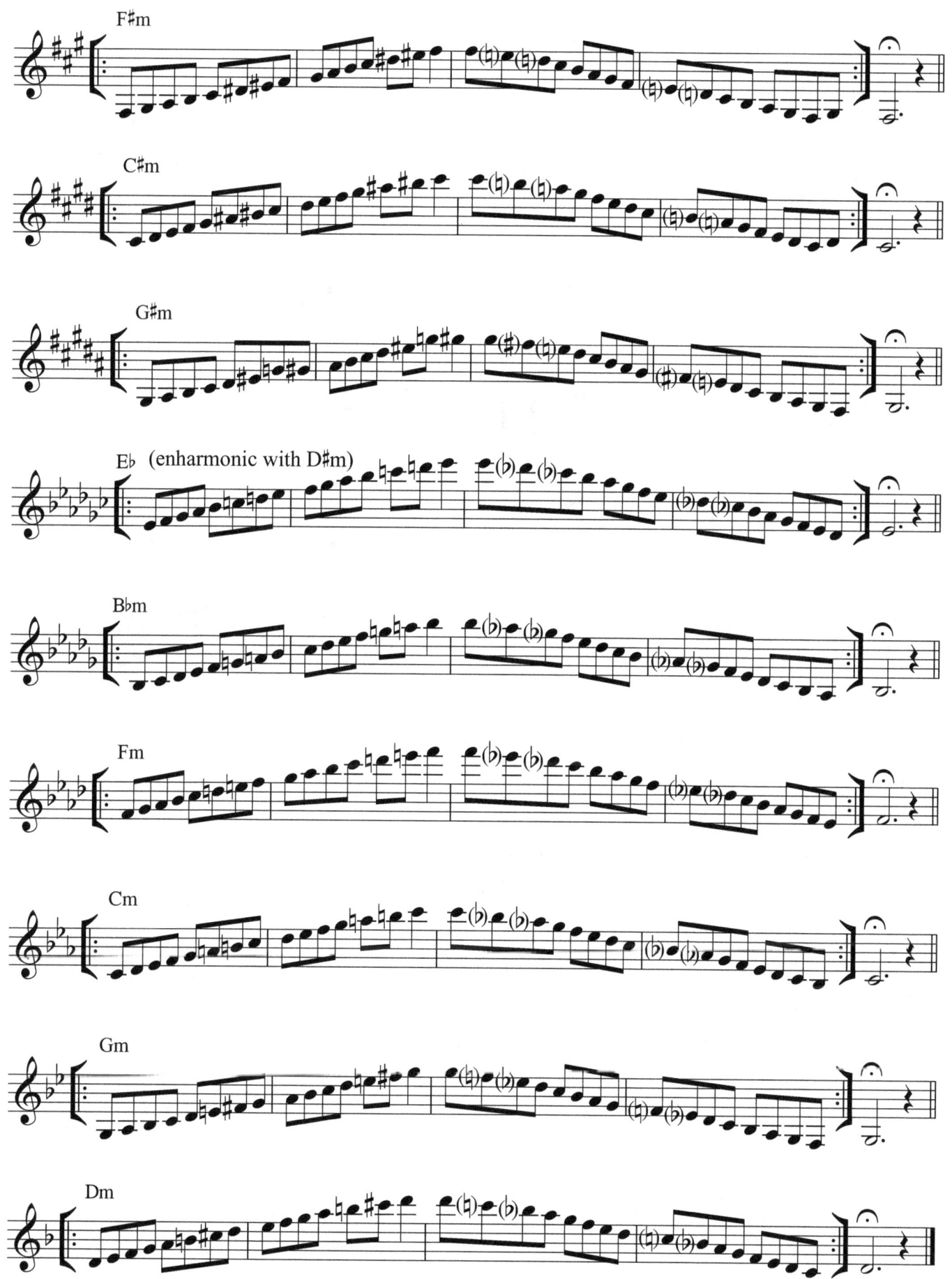

*Sounding a bit Middle Eastern.....*

# The 12 Harmonic Minor scales - One octave

minor scale with raised 7th degree - both ascending and descending

# The 12 Melodic minor Scales - Two Octaves

minor scale with raised 7th degree -both ascending and descending

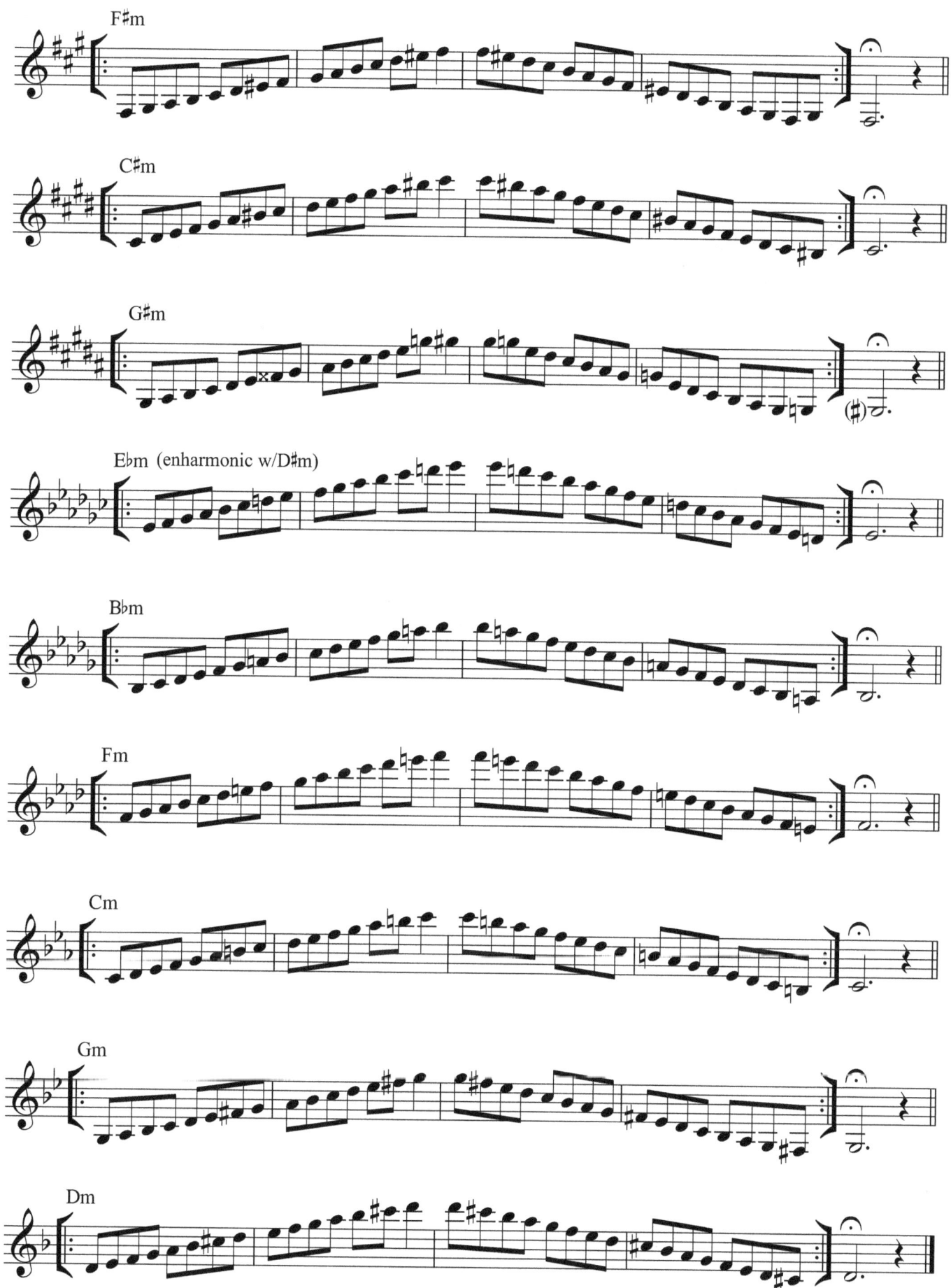

23

© 2012 Improve Your Game - JGMusik ApS DK

*This will mess your brain up*

# Chromatic Exercise 1 - One Octave

Please read "Introduction to chapters" for reference - see index

## Middle Register

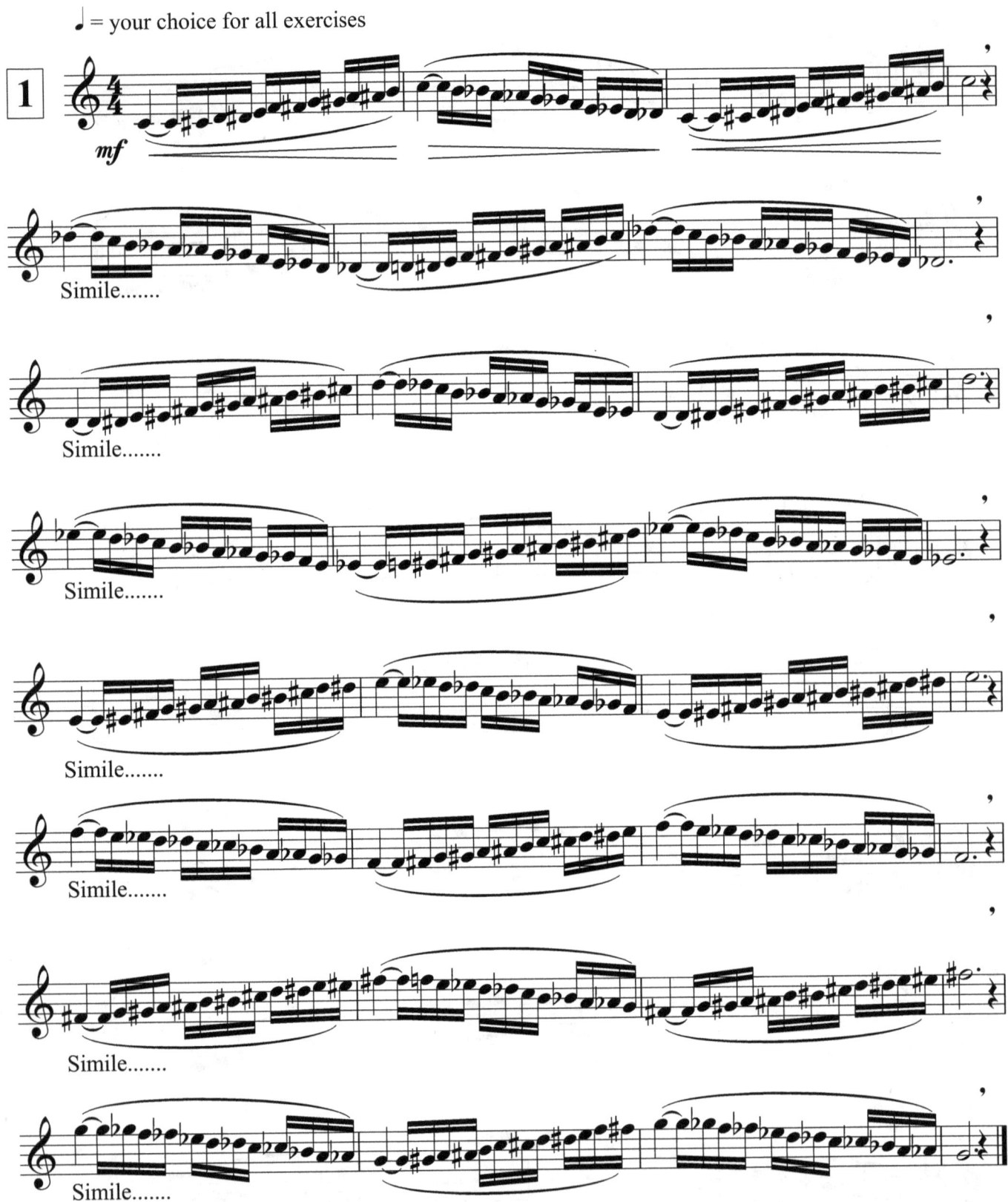

## High Register

© 2012 Improve Your Game - JGMusik ApS DK

26

Low Register

3

mf

Simile.......

Simile.......

Simile.......

Simile.......

Simile.......

Simile.......

Simile.......

# Chromatic Exercise 2 - Triplets, One & 1/2 Octave

## Middle Register

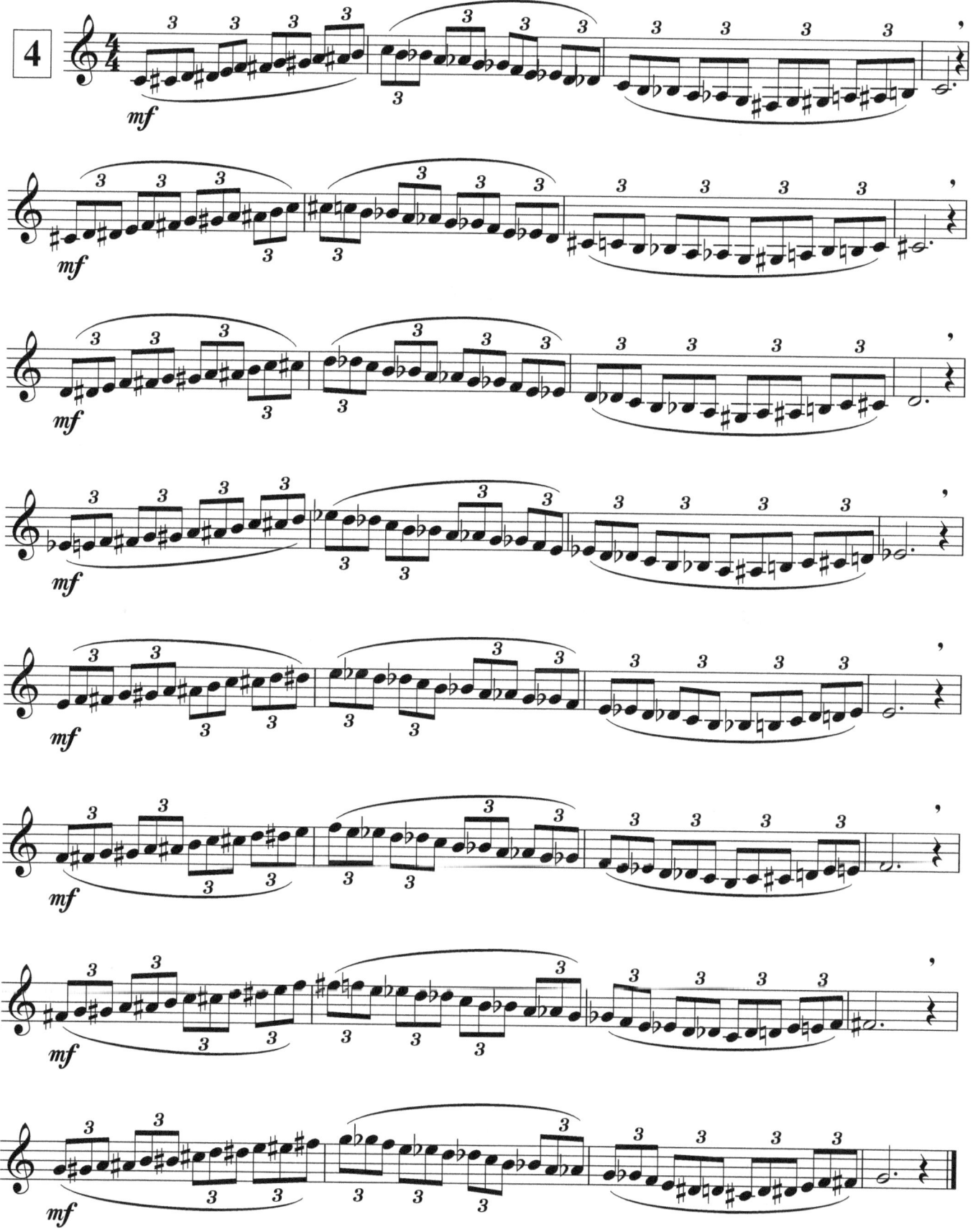

28

**High Register**

Play only if within your range

5

## Chromatic Exercise 3 - One Octave In Circle of 5ths

### Middle Register

30

# High Register

Play only if within your range

# Low Register

## Chromatic Exercise 4 - Two Octaves, Chromatic

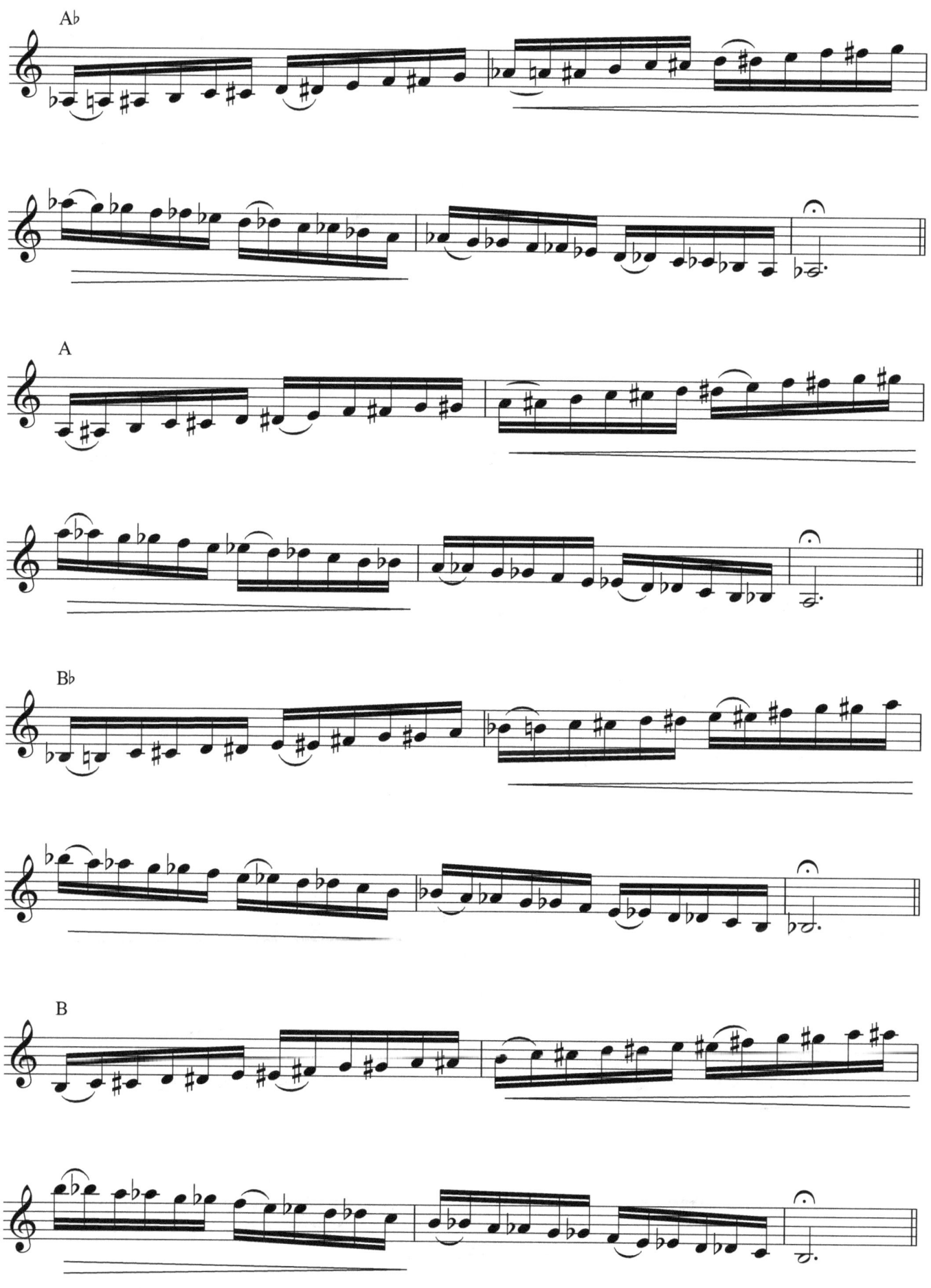

# Moving Chromatic Studies

Alternative articulations exercise 1-4

Ex.1                                        Ex.2

Ex.3                                        Ex.4

♩ = your choice

**1**

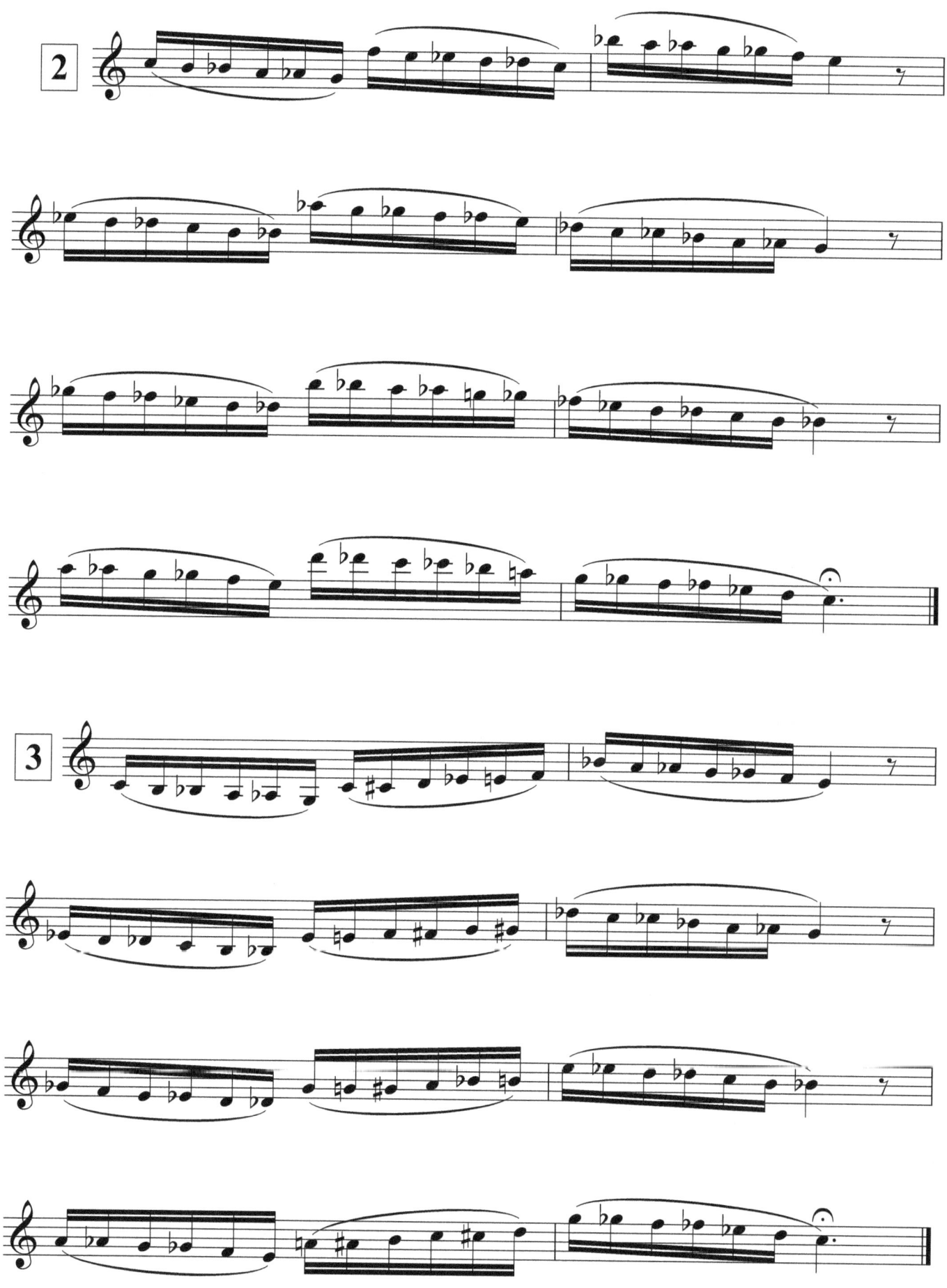

36

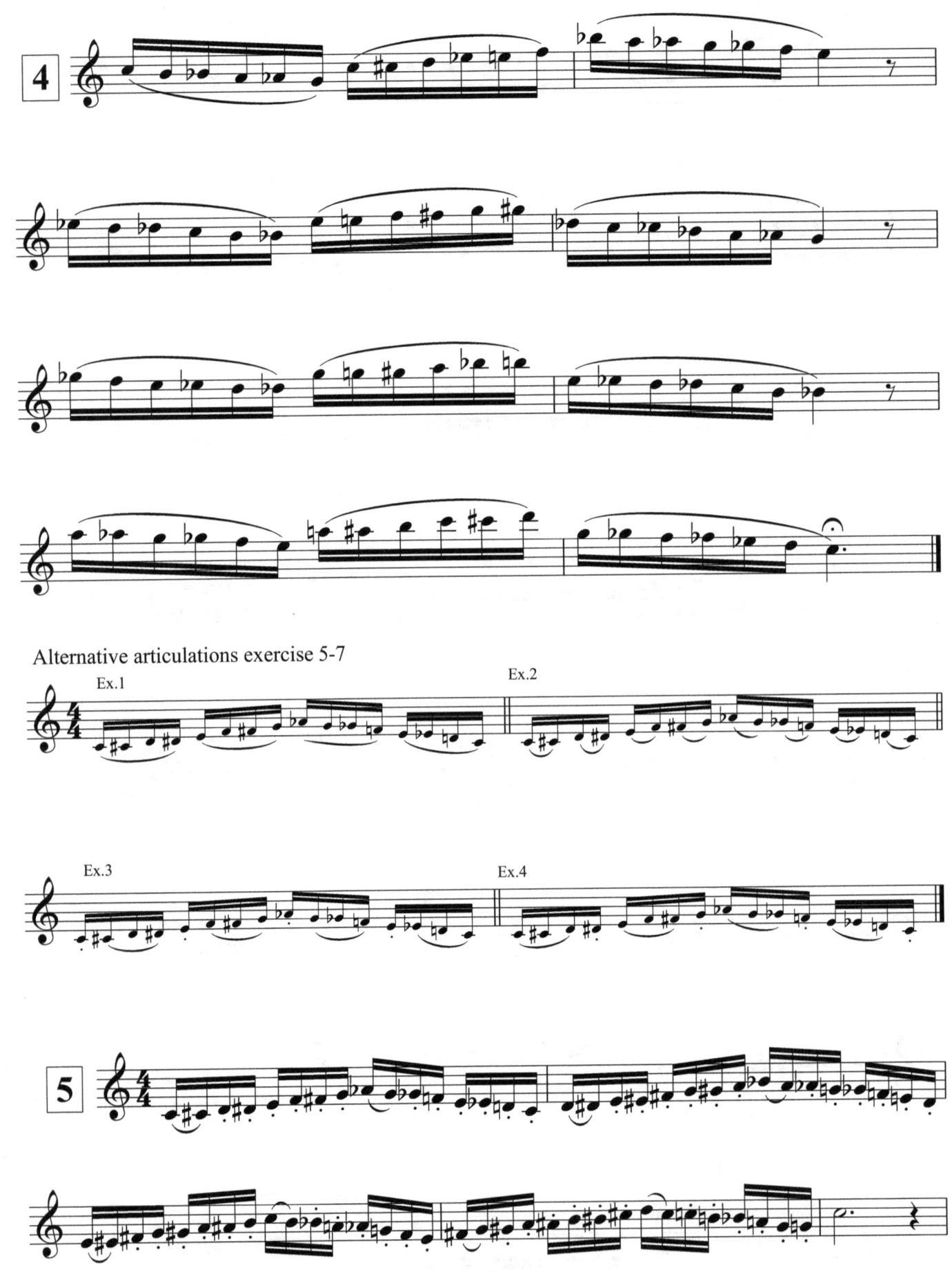

Alternative articulations exercise 5-7

38

Play only if within your range

**8**

# The Seven Modes of the Diatonic Major Scale

The next topic is HUGE!! I hate it myself, but as an old trumpet player friend told me that if you can't do anything else, you MUST know all scales and keys and play them effortlessly.

When I played in the Tivoli Boys Guard, we were taught all the normal Major and minor scales. But when I set out as a commercial player, I was introduced to the following old-fashioned names used in modern music: **Ionan, Dorian Phrygian, Lydian, Mixolydian, Aeolian and Locrian.**

To me, they sounded like characters from "Lord of the Rings". I hated the names so much that I didn't bother to learn them. Since turning 50, I've become a sucker for learning and have added these scales in my musical vocabulary. Here is a mnemonic phrase that I use to help remember the names of these scales:

**I D**on't **P**lay **L**ike **M**r. **A**rmstrong **L**ately

Note that the first letters of each word are the first letters of each scale. Pretty cool, huh? Try to come up with your own mnemonic phrase to help you remember these scales. Be creative!

Below is a breakdown of the seven modes. Take a "normal" C major scale (all the white keys on the piano from C to C). Now move it one whole step and play it from D to D. Now you have a Dorian D scale. It's a Dm scale that fits Dm6, m7 & 13 chord. At first look at the charts, but as soon as you understand it - close the book and use your head instead.

These next exercises are dedicated to these scales in all 12 keys.

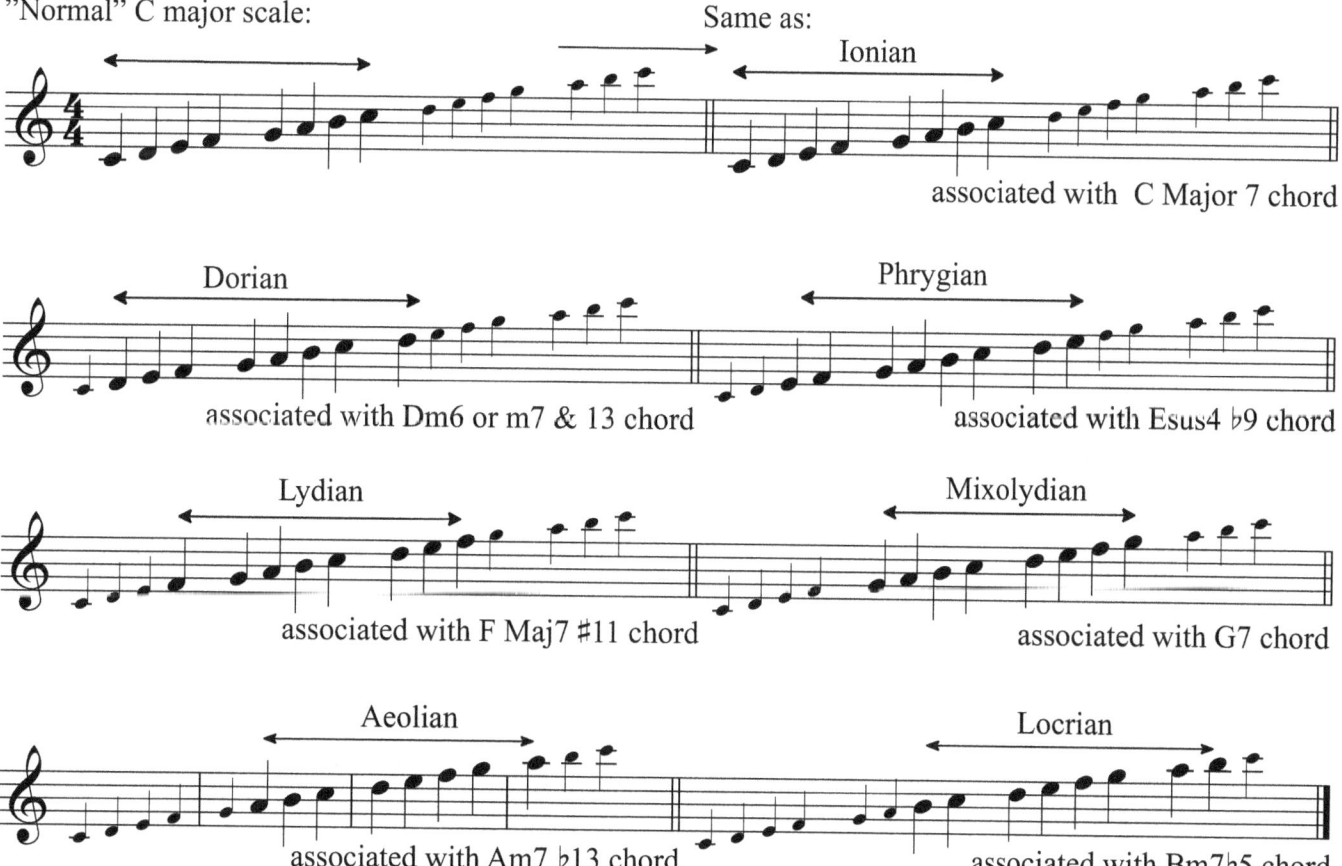

*Here we go - but this one is easy*

# The 12 Ionian Scales - One Octave

Major scale with raised 7th degree - associated with maj7 chords

1x: Slured
2x: Tenuto
3x: Staccato

**F#**

Simile...

**G**

Simile...

**Ab**

Simile...

**A**

Simile...

**Bb**

Simile...

**B**

Simile...

# The 12 Ionian Scales - Two Octaves

Major scale with raised 7th degree - associated with maj7 chords

1x: Slured
2x: Tenuto

C

Db

Simile...

D

Simile...

Eb

Simile...

E

Simile...

F

Simile...

**F#**

Simile...

**G**

Simile...

**A♭**

Simile...

**A**

Simile...

**B♭**

Simile...

**B**

Simile...

# The 12 Dorian Scales - One Octave

minor scale with low 7th degree - associated with minor 6,7 and 13 chords

1x: Slured
2x: Tenuto
3x: Staccato

Simile.......

Simile.......

Simile.......

Simile.......

Simile.......

**F#**

Simile.......

**G**

Simile.......

**A♭**

Simile.......

**A**

Simile.......

**B♭**

Simile.......

**B**

Simile.......

# The 12 Dorian Scales - Two Octaves

minor scale with low 7th degree - associated with minor 6,7 and 13 chords

1x: Slured
2x: Tenuto

# The 12 Phrygian Scales - One Octave

minor scale with lowered 2nd, 6th and 7th degree - associated with sus4 and b9 chords

1x: Slured
2x: Tenuto
3x: Staccato

**F#**

Simile.......

**G**

Simile.......

**G#**

Simile.......

**A**

Simile.......

**Bb**

Simile.......

**B**

# The 12 Phrygian Scales - Two Octaves

minor scale with lowered 2nd ,6th and 7th degree - associated with sus4 and b9 chords

1x: Slured
2x: Tenuto

**F# Phrygian**

**G Phrygian**

**G# Phrygian**

**A Phrygian**

**Bb Phrygian**

**B Phrygian**

# The 12 Lydian Scales - One Octave

Major scale with raised 4th and 7th degree - associated with maj7, # 11 chords

1x: Slured
2x: Tenuto
3x: Staccato

52

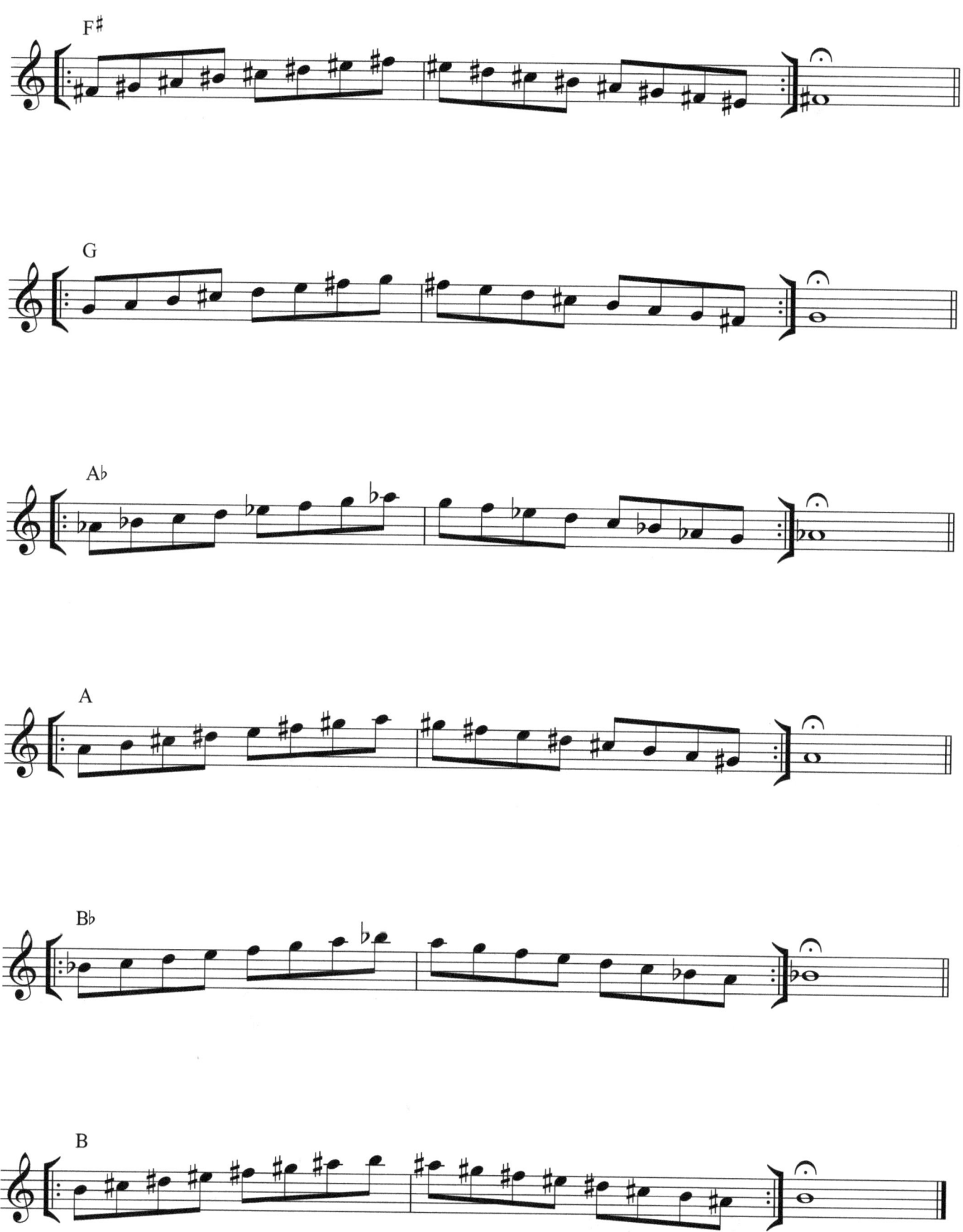

# The 12 Lydian Scales - Two Octaves

Major scale with raised 4th and 7th degree - associated with maj7, # 11 chords

1x: Slured
2x: Tenuto

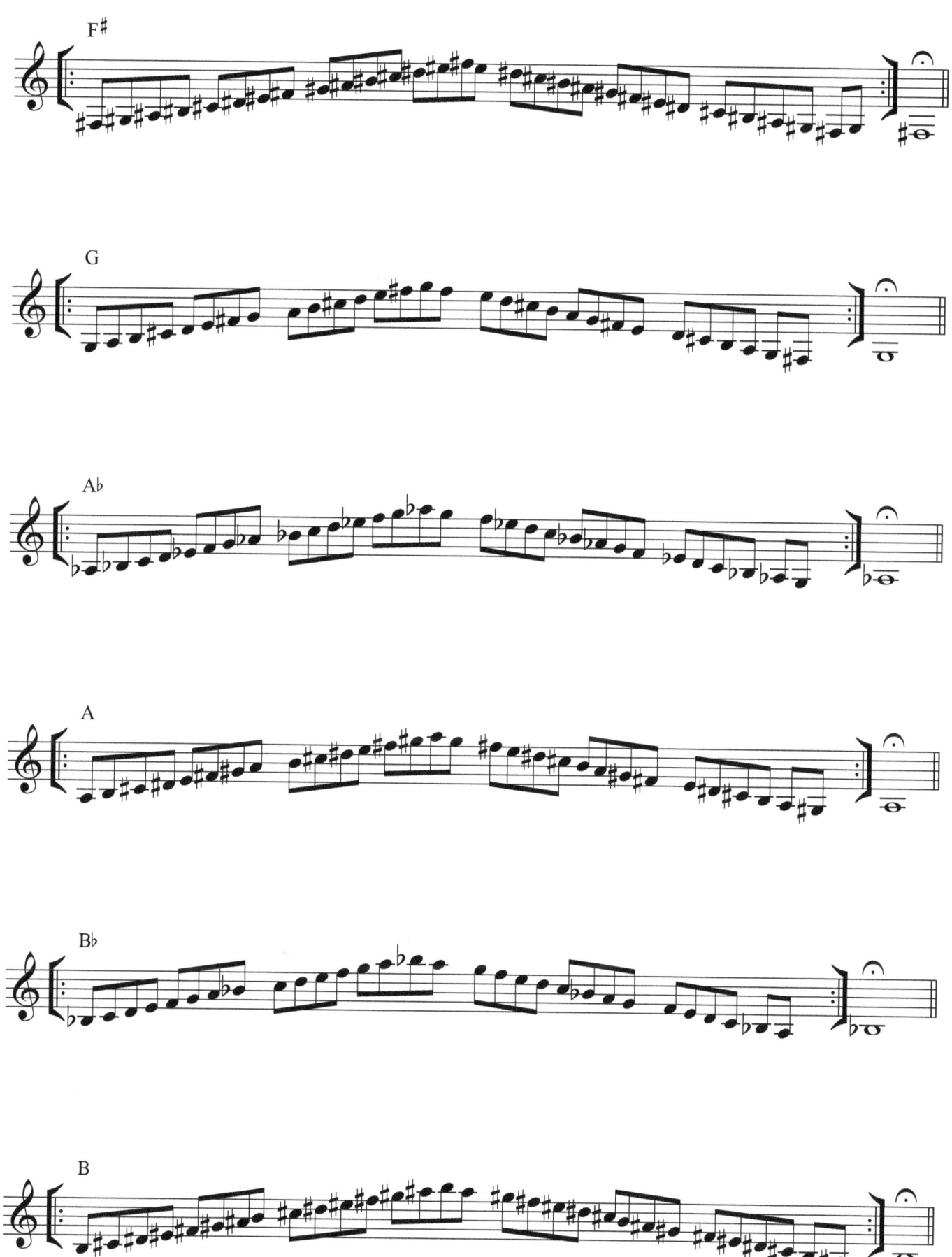

# The 12 Mixolydian Scales - One Octave

Minor scale with lowered 7th degree

1x: Slured
2x: Tenuto
3x: Staccato

Simile...

Simile...

Simile...

Simile...

F#

Simile...

G

Simile...

Ab

Simile...

A

Simile...

Bb

B

Simile...

# The 12 Mixolydian Scales - Two Octaves

Minor scale with lowered 7th degree

1x: Slured
2x: Tenuto

# The 12 Aeolian Scales - One Octave

minor scale with lowered 6th and 7th degree- associated with m7, b13 chords

1x: Slured
2x: Tenuto
3x: Staccato

**F#**

simile...

**G**

simile...

**A♭**

simile...

**A**

simile...

**B♭**

simile...

**B**

simile...

# The 12 Aeolian Scales - Two Octaves

minor scale with lowered 6th and 7th degree- associated with m7, b13 chords

1x: Slured
2x: Tenuto

simile...

simile...

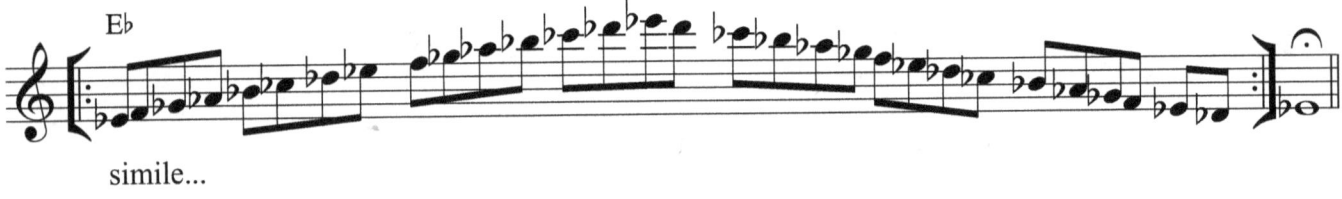

simile...

simile...

simile...

**F#**

*simile...*

**G**

*simile...*

**Ab**

*simile...*

**A**

*simile...*

**Bb**

*simile...*

**B**

*simile...*

# The 12 Locrian Scales - One Octave

minor scale with low 2nd, 5th, 6th and 7th step - associated with m7, b5 chords

1x: Slured
2x: Tenuto
3x: Staccato

**F#**

simile...

**G**

simile...

**G#**

simile...

**A**

simile...

**Bb**

simile...

**B**

simile...

# The 12 Locrian Scales - Two Octaves

minor scale with lowered 2nd, 5th, 6th and 7th step - associated with m7, b5 chords

1x: Slured
2x: Tenuto

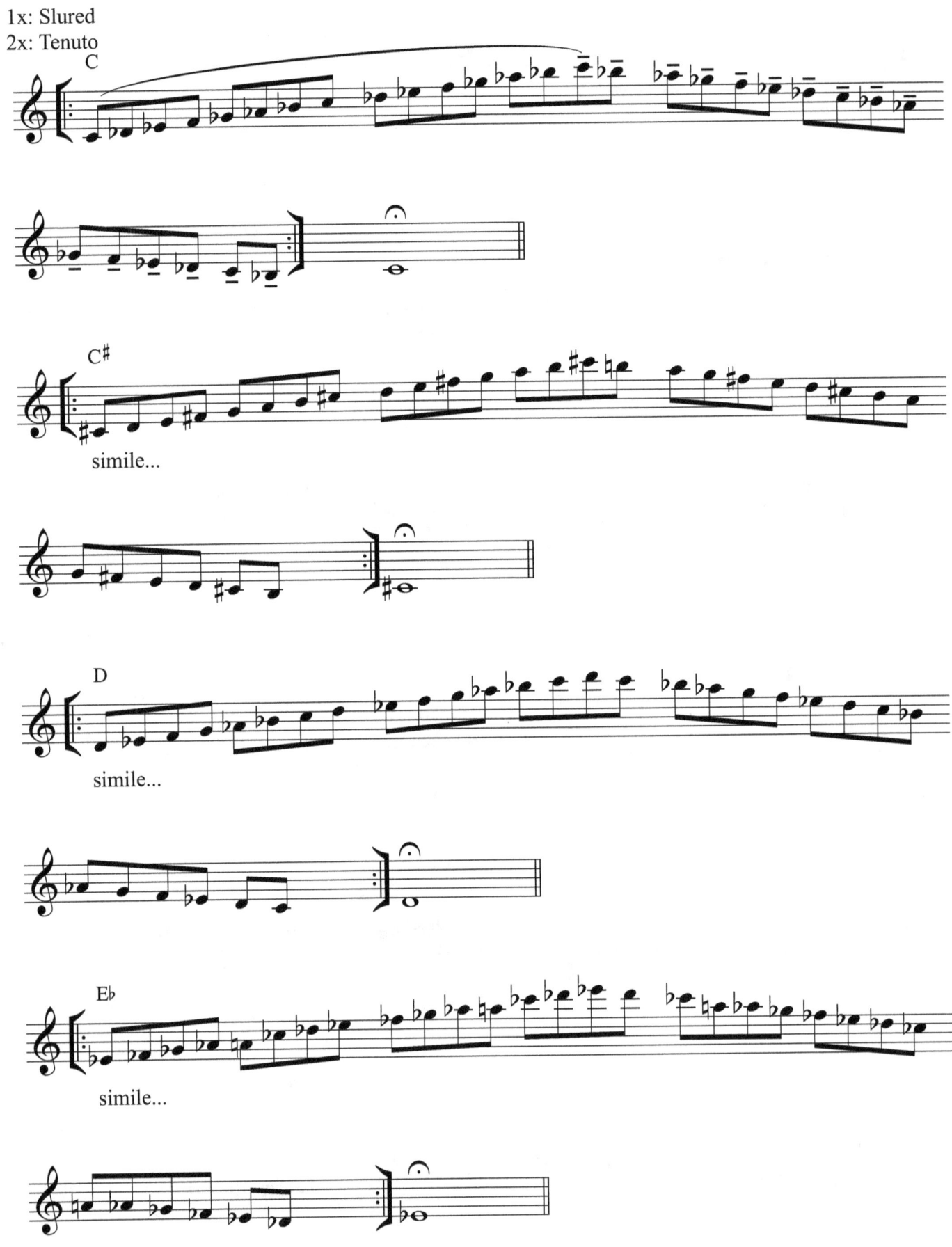

68

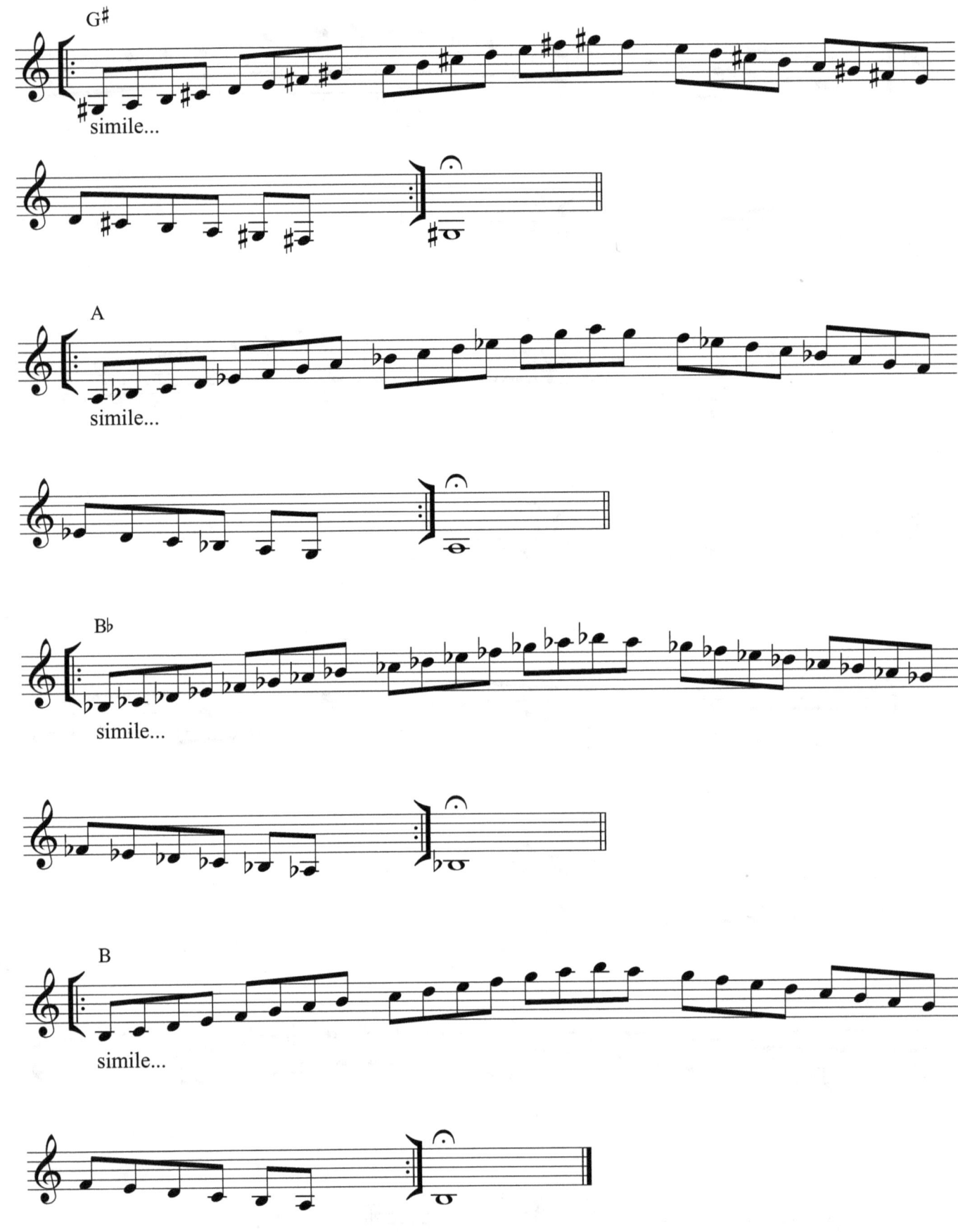

That's it!!! - You're through - BUT!!!!!!!!!..........

# WISE TRUMPET TAPAS - "FUNNY"

How do trumpet players traditionally greet each other?

"Hi . Nice to meet you. I'm better than you."

Four trumpet players are in a minivan. The minivan goes off a cliff. What's the tragedy in this? You can fit 8 trumpet players in a minivan.

How do you improve the aerodynamics of a trumpet player's car? Take the Domino's Pizza sign off the roof.

Why does a trumpet have three valve? Because trumpet players can't count to four!!

Why can't a gorilla play trumpet? It's too sensitive.

What's the difference between trumpet players and government bonds? Government bonds eventually mature and earn money.

What's the difference between a trumpet and a chain saw? Vibrato, though you can minimize this difference by holding the chain saw very still.

What is a gentleman? Somebody who knows how to play trumpet - but doesn't

When in doubt, add a shake!!

# First 12 Octatonic Scales - One Octave

Diminished scale (half step-whole step) - associated with diminished chords

1x: Slured
2x: Tenuto
3x: Staccato

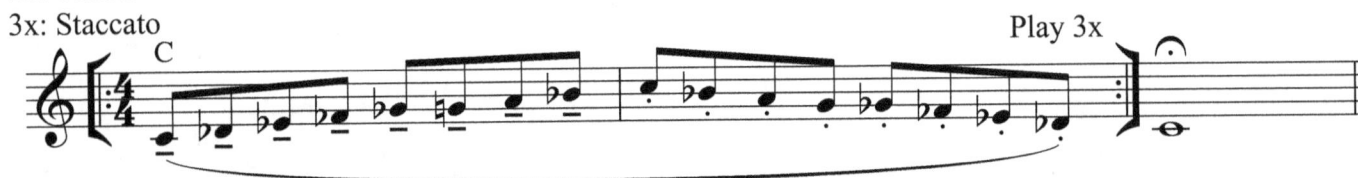

# First 12 Octatonic Scales - Two Octaves

Diminished scale (half step-whole step) - associated with diminished chords

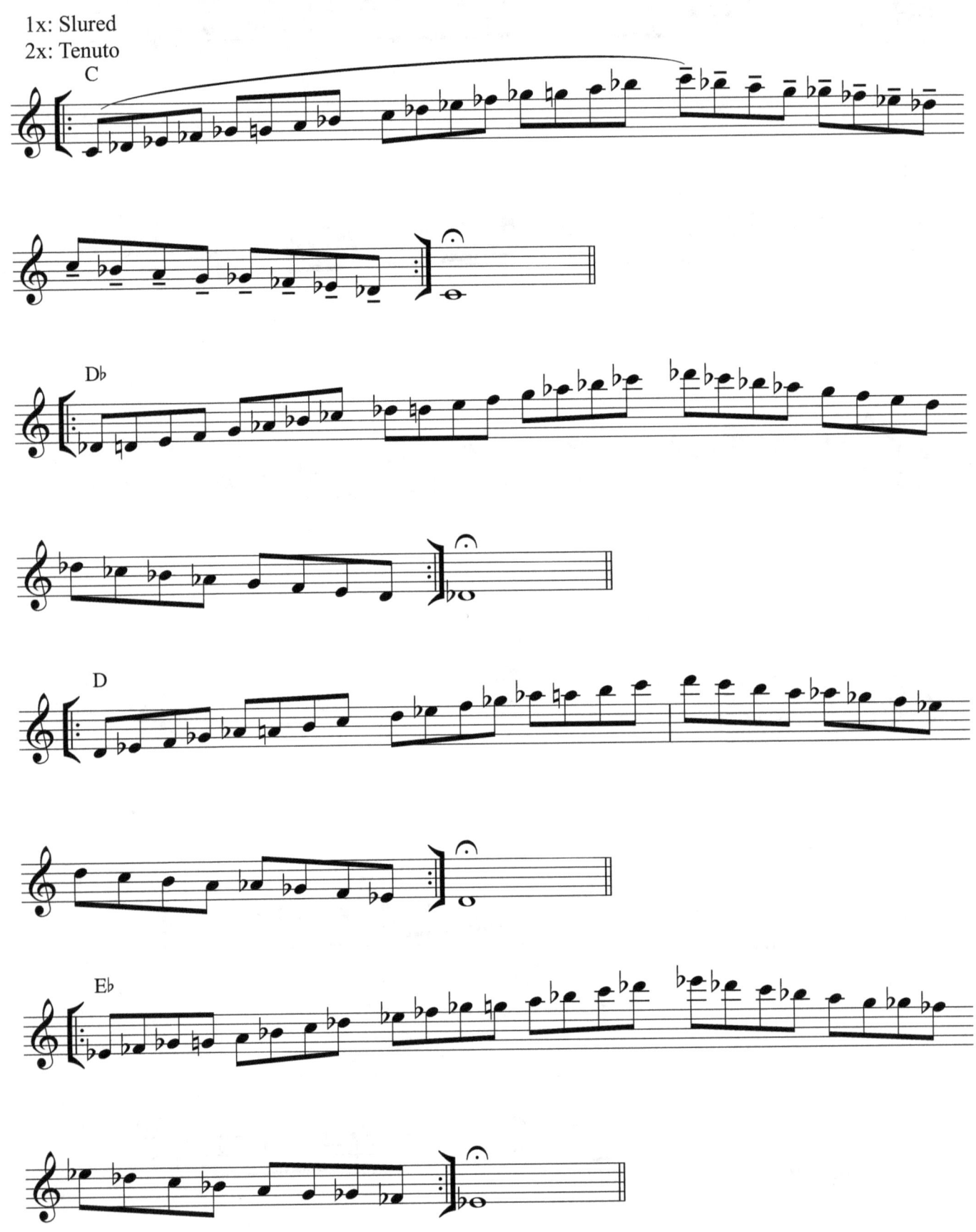

1x: Slured
2x: Tenuto

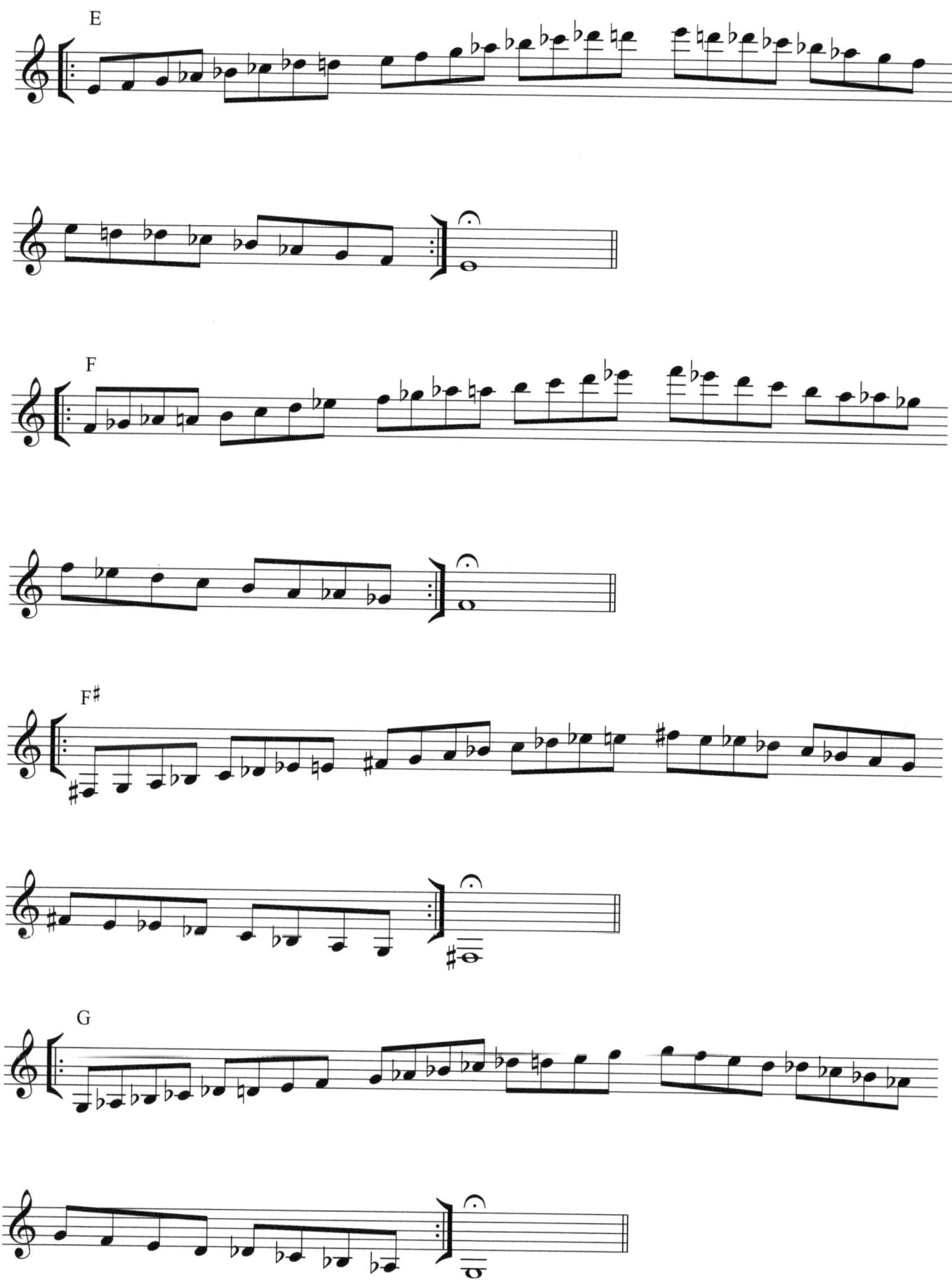

74

# Second 12 Octatonic Scales - One Octave

### Diminished scale (whole step-half step) - associated with diminished chords

1x: Slured
2x: Tenuto
3x: Staccato

**F#**

*simile...*

**G**

*simile...*

**A♭**

*simile...*

**A**

*simile...*

**B♭**

*simile...*

**B**

*simile...*

# Second 12 Octatonic Scales - Two Octaves

Diminished scale (whole step-half step) - associated with diminished chords

1x: Slured
2x: Tenuto

**C**

**D♭**

simile...

**D**

simile...

**E♭**

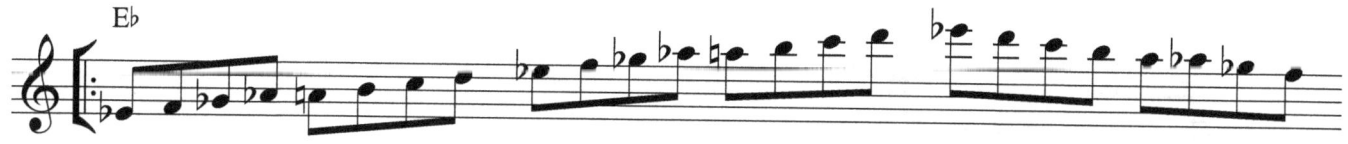

simile...

simile...

simile...

simile...

simile...

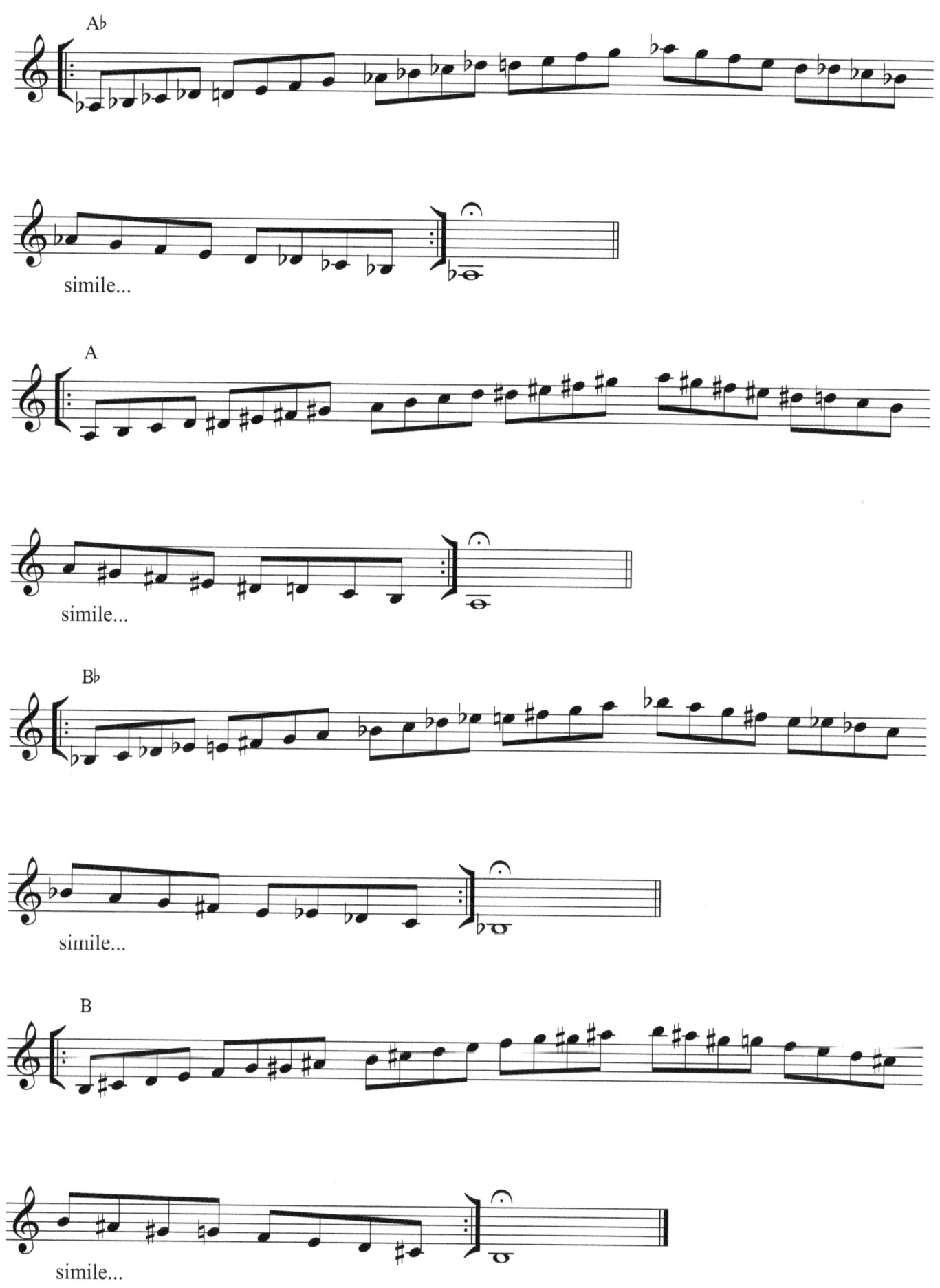

simile...

simile...

simile...

simile...

# The 12 Wholetone Scales - One Octave

(whole-tone-whole-tone) - associated with dominant 7#5 chords

1x: Slured
2x: Tenuto
3x: Staccato

F#

*simile...*

G

*simile...*

Ab

*simile...*

A

*simile...*

Bb

*simile...*

B

*simile...*

# The 12 Wholetone Scales - Two Octave

(whole-tone-whole-tone) - associated with dominant 7#5 chords

1x: Slured
2x: Tenuto

*I promise - after tomorrow it feels easier.*

# Glaesels "Brainboiler" - Major

### Please read "Introduction to chapters" for reference - see index

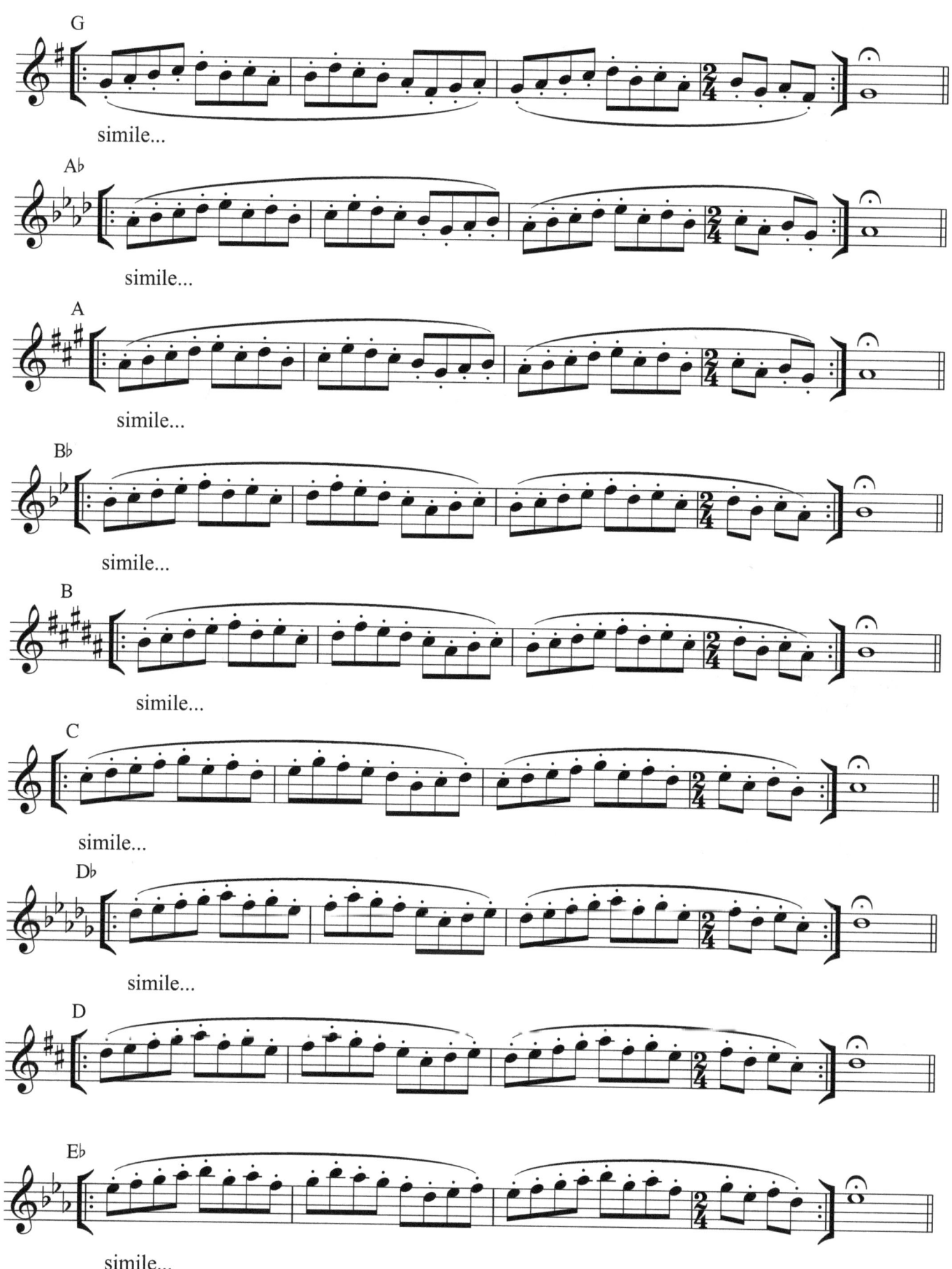

**E**

simile...

**F**

simile...

## Soften your embouchure by playing these low versions

**B**

simile...

**B♭**

simile...

**A**

simile...

**A♭**

simile...

**G**

simile...

# Glaesels "Brainboiler" - minor

88

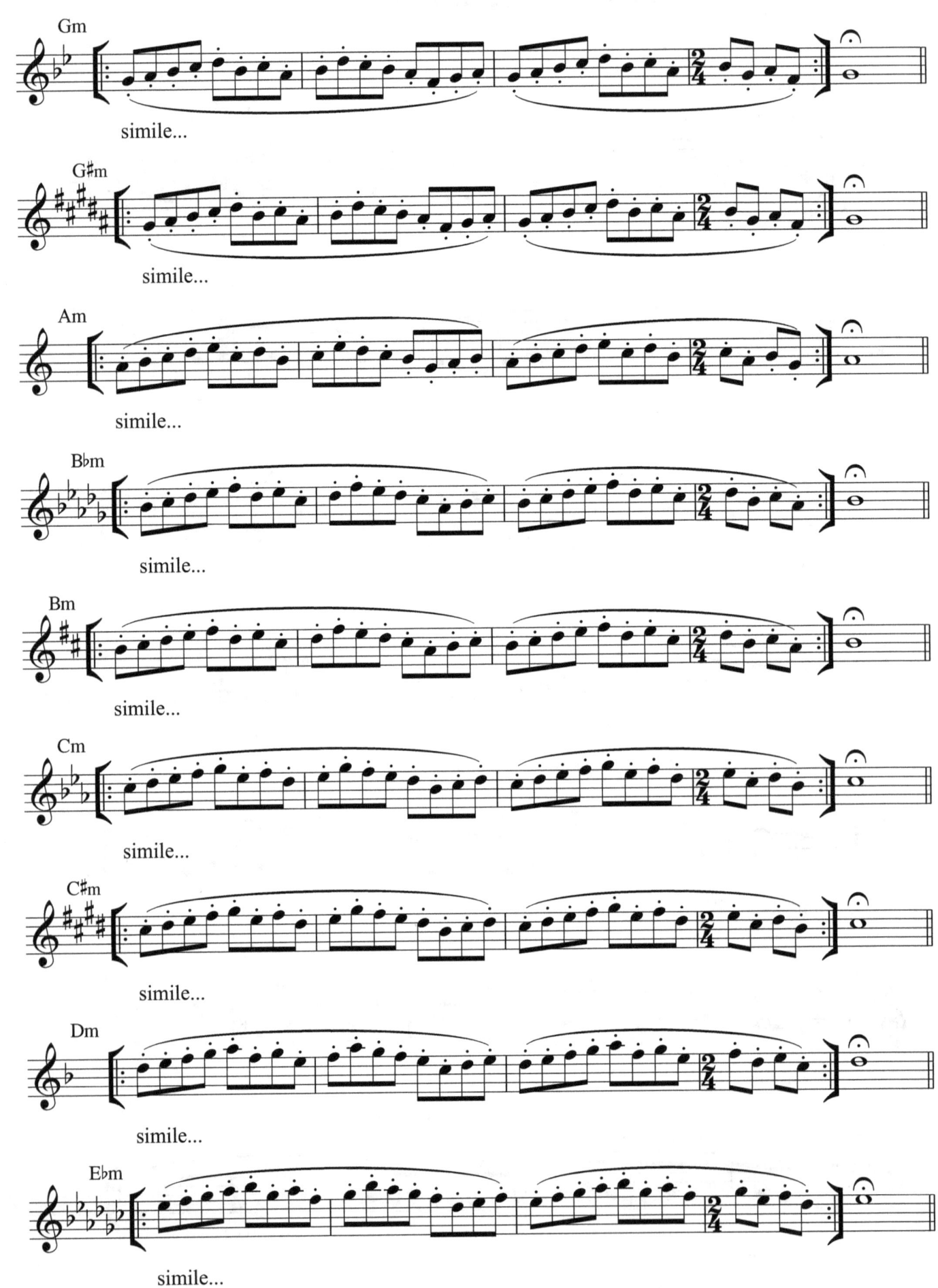

*simile...*

*simile...*

## Soften you embrochure by playing these low versions

*simile...*

*simile...*

*simile...*

*simile...*

*Let's get dizzy!!*

# Glaesel "Brainboiler" - Whole-note

92

## Soften your embouchure by playing these low versions

# Two Alternative "Brainboiler" Themes

### Please read "Introduction to chapters" for reference - see index

*Note - Diminished version not possible.

*Repetition is the mother of skill*

# Dexterity Exercises - Level 1

Please read also "Introduction to chapters" for reference - see index

This exercise looks looooooong and boring. Well, you know what? It is!!! But the scary part is actually finding out how difficult it is simply to repeat a sequence of fingerings - over and over again. This exercise strenghtens your dexterity as well as improving your stamina.

We start with 1/8-note triplets, proceed to 1/16-notes , and then on from there. I only write up to a quintuplet, but you can expand rhythmically if you're into it. Go for it!!!

In Exercise 14 we expand to two octaves. Remember - if you don't get it in 3 strikes - you're out. Eventually you will succeed - I promise!

Do yourself a favor. Thoroughly understand the concept of each exercise.  Then close the book (and your eyes) and focus on your fingers. If you have to read all exercises, this chapter will be a pain in the "@#*%#@"!

Spread the different rhythms out over your week or just take 2-3 each day so you don't get crazy. 1/8-note triplets on Monday, 1/16-notes on Tuesday,  etc..

TIP!! To get the most out of these exercises, "bang" the valves down so shifting between notes becomes as distinct as possible.

95

simile........

simile........

© 2012 Improve Your Game - JGMusik ApS DK

96

98

**Expanding to two octaves. Remember - *3 strikes and you're out!!***

100

Take a nice long break and play something meaningful.

*I'll have you committedto this before Level 3*
# Dexterity Exercises - Level 2

It still looks looooong and boring - and it still is. We started with 1/8-note triplets so now we go on to 1/16 notes.

In Exercise 14 we go again expand to two octaves. Remember again - if you don't get it in three attempts - you're out. Eventually you will succeed - I promise!!

Do yourself a favor. Thoroughly understand the concept of each exercise. Then close the book (and your eyes) and focus on your fingers. If you have to read all exercises, this chapter will be a pain in the "@#%*$@$@"!

TIP!! To get the most out of these exercises, "bang" the valves down so shifting between notes becomes so destinct as possible.

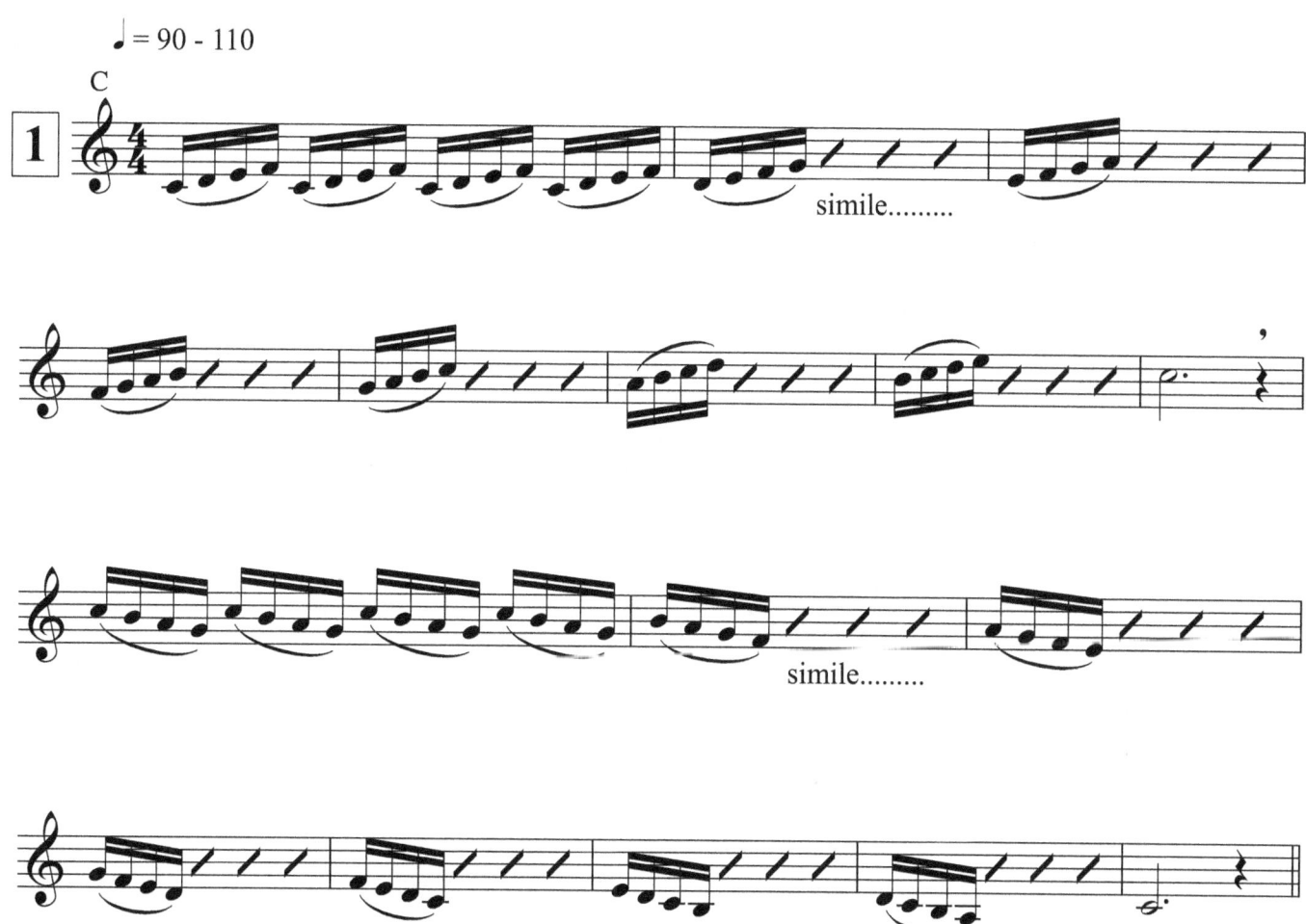

104

106

**Expand to two octaves. Remember - 3 strikes and you're out!!**

110

112

Take a well-deserved break. Then play something beautiful.

# Dexterity Exercises -level 3

Still long and boring. But necessary. So on to quintuplets.

In Exercise 9 we expand to two octaves. Remember - if you don't get it in three attempts - you're out. Eventually you will succeed - I promise!!

Do yourself a favor. Thoroughly understand the concept of each exercise. Then close the book (and your eyes) and focus on your fingers. If you have to read all exercises, this chapter will be a real pain in the tukos.

Spread the different groupings over your week or just take 2-3 each day, so you don't get crazy. 1/8 triplets monday, 1/16 tuesday etc..

TIP!! To get the most out of these exercises "bang" the valves down so shift between notes becomes so destinct as possible.

114

116

Expand to two octaves. Remember - *3 strikes and you're out!*

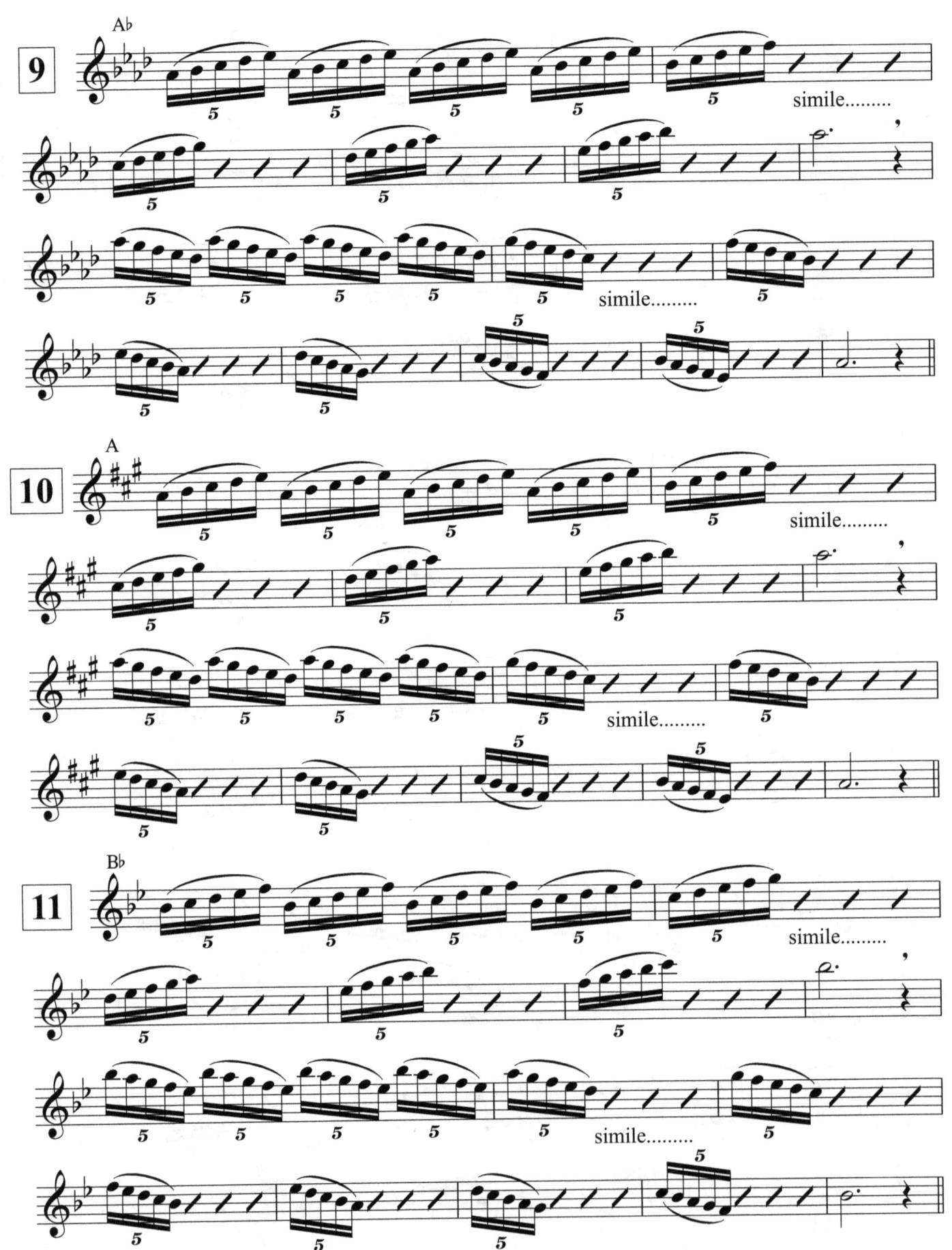

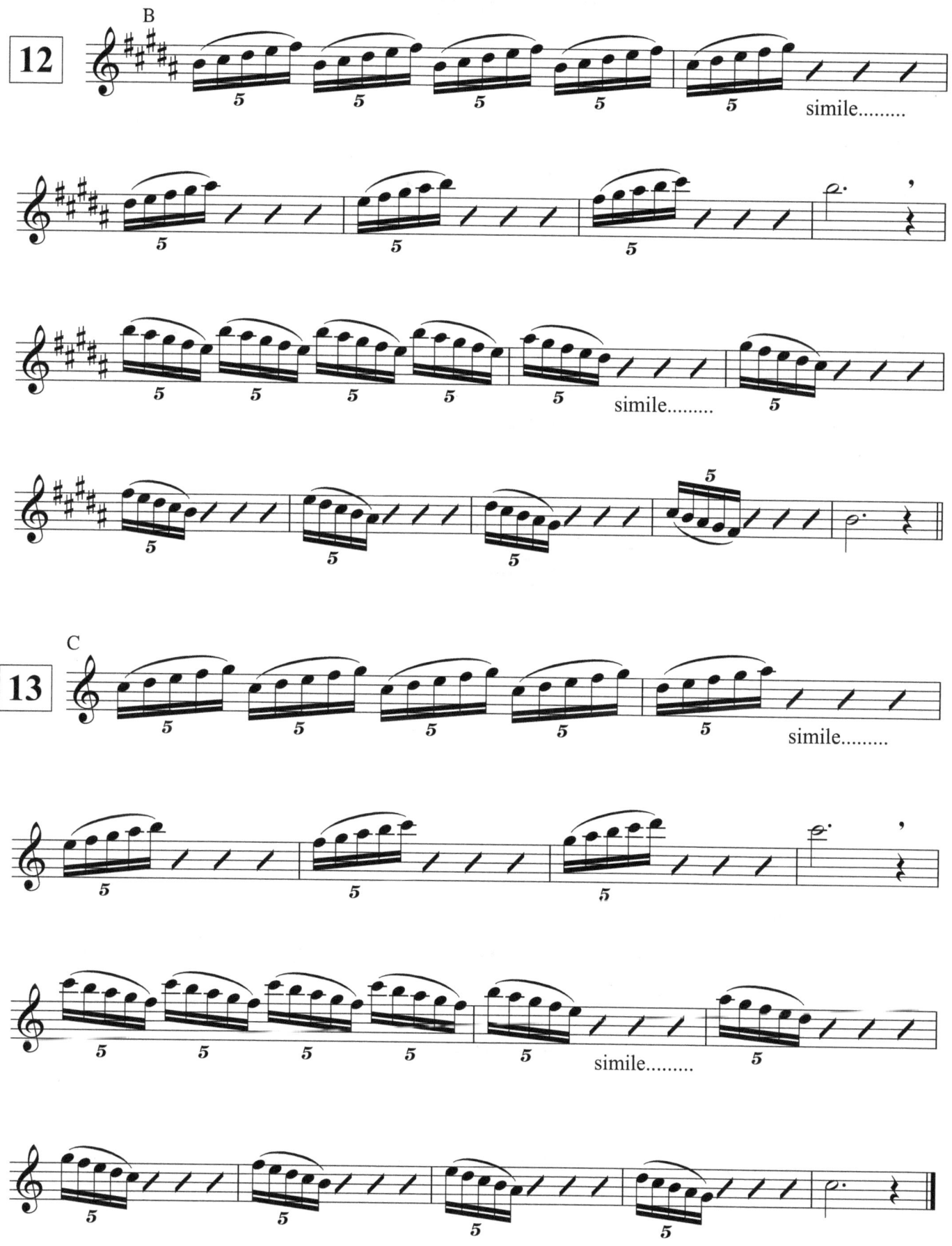

Thank you for completing this - you're a trouper!

*Dedicated to Nikolaj Viltoft - friend and trumpetplayer at the Royal Dansih opera*

# Etude For A Mentor - Eb major

Jan Glaesel

Vivace con spirituoso

# Etude Pittoresque - E minor

Jan Glaesel

© 2012 Improve Your Game - JGMusik ApS DK

*Dedicated to my good friend and trumpet player Gary Cordell - Las Vegas Nevada*

# Etude for A Friend - C minor

Jan Glaesel

## MY BOOKSHELF OF CONSTANT INSPIRATION

When I started to practice for real in 2004 the only method-book I had was:

## J.S. ARBAN - COMPLETE CONSERVATORY METHOD FOR TRUMPET

This was the book I was handed back in 1967 when I join the Tivoli Boys Guard here in Copenhagen. I think it is considered one of the "bibles" for many trumpet players. In 2004 when I began my new journey I started collecting all kinds of trumpet method books. Here is a list of the content of "My bookshelf of constant inspiration", in random order.

| Author | Title | Publisher |
| --- | --- | --- |
| J.B. Arban | Complete Conservatory Method for Trumpet | Carl Fischer |
| Herbert L. Clarke | Technical Studies for the Cornet | Carl Fischer |
| Arturo Sandoval | Playing techniques & Performance Studies Vol. 1-3 | Hal Leonard |
| James Stamp | Warm-Ups & Studies | Editions BIM |
| Claude Gordon | Systematic Approach to Daily Practice | Carl Fischer |
| Allen Vizzutti | The Allen Vizzutti Trumpet Method Vol. 1-3 | Alfred Publishing |
| Geoff Winstead | The Real Way to Play the Cat Anderson Method | GWM Publishing |
| Carmine Caruso | Musical Calisthenics for Brass | Hal Leonard |
| Max Schlossberg | Daily Drills & Technical Studies for Trumpet | M. Baron Company |
| Gabriel Parés Parés | Scales for Cornet or Trumpet | Rubank - Hal Leonard |
| J.L. Small | 27 Melodious and Rhythmical Exercises | Carl Fischer |
| David Vining | Ear training for Trumpet | Carl Fischer |
| John McNeil | Jazz Trumpet Techniques | Studio P/R |
| Charles Colin | Advanced Lip Flexibilities Vol. 1-3 | Charles Colin Music |
| Charles Colin | Complete Modern Method for Trumpet or Cornet | Charles Colin Music |
| Jon Gorrie | High notes, Low Notes and Everything in Between | www.jongorrie.com |

I've worked with all of these books and found, through them, inspiration for my own approach to trumpet playing. I pay my deepest respects to all of the writers, and it's with the utmost humility I've used them as inspiration for my version of the ultimate Trumpet Method Book.

## MUSICAL STUDIES & ETUDES:

Musical studies and etudes are just as important as technical studies. Below you will find some of my favorite collections from my bookshelf. I divide my time between Technical Studies, Musical Studies and Etudes 50/50 - I urge you to do the same.

| Author | Title | Publisher |
| --- | --- | --- |
| Sigmund Hering | Thirty Etudes for Trumpet or Cornet | Carl Fischer |
| Sigmund Hering | Thirty-two Etudes for Trumpet or Cornet | Carl Fischer |
| Sigmund Hering | Forty Progressive Etudes for Trumpet | Carl Fischer |
| Kopprasch | Sixty Selected Studies for Trumpet | Carl Fischer |
| H. Voxman | H. Selected Studies for Cornet or Trumpet | Rubank - Hal Leonard |
| H. Voxman | H. Selected Duets for Cornet or Trumpet Vol. 1-2 | Rubank - Hal Leonard |
| H. Voxman | Concert&Contest Collection for Cornet or Trumpet | Rubank - Hal Leonard |
| Larry Clark | Progressive Duets for Trumpet in Bb Vol. 1-2 | Carl Fischer |
| Walter Beeler | Solos for the Trumpet-Player | G. Schirmer - Hal Leonard |

## CREDITS:

Most of all I want, I want thank my loving wife Miriam and the rest of my family for enduring the "awful" sound of practising the trumpet - Thanks guys!!

A special thanks goes to my good friend, and fellow trumpet player **Gary Cordell,** Las Vegas Nevada, for proofreading this project. Also thank you for introducing me to Tony Scodwell.

**Tony Scodwell** - my good friend and fellow trumpet player, for letting me play one of his fantastic handmade trumpets. "Tony - you're a true artist and craftsman building your fantastic horns."

**Bob Reeves** - mouthpieces. Thank you for taking almost a day out of your busy schedule to guide me to the mouthpieces which are going to follow me, for the rest of my life.

**Jon Gorrie** - for opening my eyes to the Print On Demand concept. Also for helping me setting up the whole online marketing side of the project - Let's do something more together.

**Krogstrup & Hede** - web bureau. For always doing your best for my websites.

**Bithiah & Patrick Poulsen** - Layout. I love the cover and all your input - thank you.

**The Danish Musical Directors Union** - for financial support.

Please feel free to contact me with feedback or questions at info@trumpetgame.com